Further Praise for *The Conductive Organization*

"An evocative account of why an organization must give more than lip service to being customer-centered and how it can implement approaches to create authentic interdependence and "generalized reciprocity" between customers, partners and stakeholders to sustain its purpose."
—**Yvon Bastien**, President and General Manager, Sanofi-Synthelabo Canada, Inc.

"Saint-Onge and Armstrong's work couldn't have come at a better time. In an era of growing institutional failure and emphasis on transparency, **The Conductive Organization** provides a blueprint for creating organizations that are truly calibrated to customer needs, reliant on value-based relationships with stakeholders, and centered on knowledge capital. An accessible read, based on theory but long on practice, this book challenges us all to rethink strategies for how organizations can exceed expectations."
—**Leif Edvinsson**, The world's first director of Intellectual Capital, The world's first holder of a professorship on Intellectual Capital, Lund University, Sweden, 1998 "Brain of the Year"

"**The Conductive Organization** is that delightful rarity among management books: a distillation of the wisdom of two obviously deeply self-reflective practitioners crafted in large measure around the experiences of their own organizations but conveyed through the means of a powerful and pervasive conceptual structure that will make academics and consultants blush with envy. And, yes, for those managers who truly want to understand why knowledge is the ultimate organizational asset and how to leverage it, this is the "must read" book."
—**Liam Fahey**, Partner, Leadership Forum, Inc. and Adjunct Professor, Strategic Management at Babson College

"As organizations struggle to find new ways to operate in turbulent times, Saint-Onge and Armstrong provide us with a new way of thinking—of concentrating on strategy-making not just strategies; on calibrating to the customer not just becoming client-centric; on increasing knowledge flows not just gaining knowledge. **The Conductive Organization** provides leaders at all levels with a framework that is grounded in the authors' cumulative experiences with success and shaped by their values."
—**Tom Jenkins**, CEO, Open Text

"**The Conductive Organization** presents compelling insight on organizational and knowledge strategies that leaders can take to gain a competitive advantage. The premise that a connected enterprise is empowered through conductivity puts the customer at the center. Conductivity realizes the full potential of technology, and goes way beyond it. Any leader who wants to succeed will want to put this book on their list of must reads."

—**Mary Lee Kennedy**, Director, Knowledge Network Group,
Microsoft Corporation

"Organizational success relies heavily on the capability to leverage both institutional and personal knowledge. While our systems and approaches for managing information are for the most part highly developed, we are just starting to understand the complexities of how to best utilize our personal knowledge in pursuit of organizational goals. S.A. Armstrong Limited has been at the forefront of this journey of discovery. This book provides insights coupled with practical applications that can guide any organization toward a more effective management and use of its most valuable asset- the unique knowledge of its people."

—**Maseo Maekawa**, Chairman of the Board, Mayekawa Mfg. Co., Ltd., Tokyo, Japan; President, Mayekawa Holding AG, Zug, Switzerland; President, Mycom Intertec AG, Zug, Switzerland

"This book is a personal and insightful guide for organizations wishing to better engage with the knowledge economy. It is deeply grounded in the authors own experiences, which makes their recommendations that much more cogent and sensible."

—**Laurence Prusak**, Distinguished Scholar in Residence, Babson College, USA

"My prediction is that **The Conductive Organization** will become the most conductive new idea in management circles and business schools around the world. The central idea that all organizational structures in processes must become customer dictated is currently being written about by other authors, but only as a theory. Where the authors differentiate themselves is in providing the actual organizational blue print for making customers permanent creative partners in the innovation, manufacturing, and delivery processes. **The Conductive Organization** book is a platform that will generate thousands of fruitful management practices and methods."

—**Dan Sullivan**, President, The Strategic Coach

The Conductive Organization
Building Beyond Sustainability

The Conductive Organization

Building Beyond Sustainability

Hubert Saint-Onge *and* Charles Armstrong

ELSEVIER
BUTTERWORTH
HEINEMANN

AMSTERDAM • BOSTON • HEIDELBERG • LONDON
NEW YORK • OXFORD • PARIS • SAN DIEGO
SAN FRANCISCO • SINGAPORE • SYDNEY • TOKYO

Elsevier Butterworth-Heinemann
200 Wheeler Road, Burlington, MA 01803, USA
Linacre House, Jordan Hill, Oxford OX2 8DP, UK

 Recognizing the importance of preserving what has been written, Elsevier prints its
books on acid-free paper whenever possible.

Library of Congress Cataloging-in-Publication Data
Saint-Onge, Hubert.
   The conductive organization : building beyond sustainability / Hubert Saint-Onge
and Charles Armstrong.
       p. cm.
   ISBN 0-7506-7735-X (alk. paper)
   1. Knowledge management.   2. Organizational learning.   I. Armstrong, Charles.
II. Title.
   HD30.2.S234   2004
   658.4′038–dc22

                                                                    2004005149

British Library Cataloguing-in-Publication Data
A catalogue record for this book is available from the British Library.

ISBN: 0-7506-7735-X

For information on all Butterworth-Heinemann publications
visit our website at www.bh.com

03 04 05 06 07 08 09 10 9 8 7 6 5 4 3 2 1

Printed in the United States of America

A mes parents, Roland et Cécile, qui m'ont inspiré à poursuivre mes rêves avec courage—HSO

To Sarah and David and to three generations of the Armstrong community who have discovered, developed, and lived our core values—CAA

Contents

Preface

The ideas and approaches that shaped *The Conductive Organization: Building Beyond Sustainability* evolved during a 10-year relationship between two practitioners leading markedly different types of organizations. Hubert Saint-Onge was Executive Vice President, Strategic Capabilities at Clarica Life Insurance Company (Clarica), a large organization from the financial services sector, and Charles Armstrong was, and continues to be, President, S.A. Armstrong Limited (Armstrong), a medium-sized corporation from the engineering and manufacturing sector. Despite their different sector foci, in recent years both these practitioners have grappled with the same problem—how best to configure, and lead, organizations to enable high and sustainable performance in the knowledge era. *The Conductive Organization* describes the solutions they crafted and applied within their organizations.

Intellectual Capital

When the authors first met in 1994, Hubert was head of The Leadership Center, and a vice-president, for the Canadian Imperial Bank of Commerce (CIBC), one of Canada's leading financial institutions. He was already a respected pioneering thinker in the then newly emerging discipline of intellectual capital management. Hubert was developing this field with other pioneers such as Leif Edvinsson, then of Skandia, a Swedish insurance company, and Karl-Erik

Sveiby, which had led to the articulation of a new intellectual capital model (customer, structural, and human capital components) that collectively delivered an organization's financial capital. This model would evolve into the Knowledge Capital Model, which is a key element in this book.

Saint-Onge et al.'s thinking and approaches attracted considerable interest worldwide, from conference organizers and the business press alike, most notably from *Fortune Magazine*. An article on intellectual capital, written by *Fortune* editor Thomas Stewart (now himself a respected thinker in the field and editor of the *Harvard Business Review*) first brought Hubert to the attention of Charles and prompted their first meeting. At this meeting at CIBC's Leadership Centre, they discovered congruence of thinking around the challenges ahead for organizations and an equal appetite for exploring new approaches to leadership and management.

Armstrong Challenges

At the time of their 1994 meeting, Charles was five years into his tenure as President of Armstrong, the then 61-year-old, third-generation, family-owned organization that he leads with his brother James.

With successful operations in the UK, USA, Europe, the Middle East, and Canada, there was a good amount of activity in the business in terms of structure and customer position. The brothers had rationalized the factories into centers of excellence, focused factories, and commenced much greater interdependence between the organizations than had previously existed. However, the brothers realized that Armstrong's capabilities had to be leveraged in new ways if the organization was to compete and succeed in the following years. Central to this approach would be establishing a self-initiated management team, a significant challenge in an entrepreneurial organization where the leadership had been held in three or four people and all decisions were upward directed.

Soon after the authors first met, they jointly attended a meeting in Santa Cruz, California where a group of like-minded practitioners were discussing intellectual capital and its implications in business. While there, Charles described the work under way in his organization to rearticulate its purpose and values and recognized from the response of the other attendees the potential power this work held for Armstrong. Rearticulating purpose and values was a critical component of the work at other organizations and would soon be so at Clarica.

It also became evident from this meeting and subsequent conversations that existing leadership models did not support meaningful and trusted delegation in organizations, but constricted their capacity to grow. Moreover, it was becoming painfully evident that the financial accounting systems were inadequate in accounting for the building of capability and intangibles of the business.

Business Value

In 1995, while on a plane to Montreal with Armstrong's cost accountant John Murtaugh, Charles laid out Hubert's elements of intellectual capital in a Venn diagram and began looking at the elements, but more importantly how they overlapped. This resultant was a practitioner's breakthrough. Charles realized that the interaction of the customer, structural, and human capital elements was where value is created. This realization gave structure to the ideas Hubert and Charles had first discussed a year earlier. Moreover, it directed efforts to study and understand the flows between the knowledge capital elements and the stocks of intellectual capital created.

Know Inc.

In 1997, Charles launched an organization called Know Inc. whose purpose was to create a network of thought leaders in the area of intellectual capital and provide them with a collaborative environment in which they could begin to structuralize their work, thereby making it accessible to more organizations and more people. Through the resulting toolkits, the works of practitioners such as Karl-Erik Sveiby, Valdis Krebs, and Verna Allee were made available for organizations to use on their intranets. Know Inc. also developed software to help corporations better manage their intangible assets. This ongoing collaboration between Charles and Hubert gave structure to the evolution of their thinking.

Clarica Challenges

In 1997, Hubert accepted the position of Executive Vice President, Strategic Capabilities for what was then Mutual Life of Canada. Mutual Life had a long, respected, and successful history, having provided investment and insurance solutions to Canadians since 1870. However, by the mid 1990s its leadership team had agreed that, given the speed of change and increasing competition, to further develop the organization required demutualization and the conversion to a shareholder-owned company, which it would achieve by 1999. If this wasn't enough of a change challenge, the organization was also in the throes of acquiring the Canadian operations of the insurer MetLife—an acquisition that would double Mutual's size. At the same time, becoming a stock company led to the renaming of the organization Clarica Life Insurance Company. "Clarica" was more than just a "name"; it was purposefully chosen to mean *clarity through dialogue*, which would represent the brand promise that would connect Clarica with its customers. Building this brand would become another change imperative.

Clarica Profile

With offices across Canada, Clarica served more than 3 million customers in Canada and almost a quarter of a million customers in the USA through 8,000 agents, staff, financial planners, and group representatives. Headquartered in Waterloo, Ontario (about 75 miles south west of Toronto), Clarica, provided a full range of wealth management products in addition to individual retail and group insurance. It was been named one of the top 20 knowledge management organizations worldwide.

The following quick facts help situate Clarica in the financial services industry at the time:

- Canada's first and oldest mutual insurance company.
- Insures one in ten Canadians.
- First in retail life insurance in force in the Canadian market.
- Second in Canadian market share of retail insurance (based on income from premiums).
- Largest provider of corporate loans among life-insurance-based financial institutions.
- First Canadian-based mutual life insurance company to demutualize.
- IPO of $680 million was the second largest ever on the Toronto Stock Exchange.

In May 2002, Clarica became part of Sun Life Financial and the center of Canadian operations for both organizations. At the time of the merger, Clarica's shares were trading at almost treble the price at their initial public offering, and its brand had been valued in excess of $750 million. Hubert left the company at that time, and so the work in this book is usually referred to in the past tense to reflect the point in time when Hubert was working at Clarica.

Armstrong Profile

Headquartered in Toronto, Armstrong was incorporated in 1934 under the leadership of its founder Samuel Allan Armstrong and remains a privately owned company. With over 600 employees worldwide, operating six manufacturing plants on two continents, it's globally recognized as a leader and innovator in design, engineering, and manufacturing within the fluid flow equipment industry. Its products are internationally recognized for design efficiency, long service life, and operating economy. Products include: commercial pumps, residential and light commercial hydronics, and fire pumps. These products are used in residential, commercial, and industrial installations in some of the world's premier facilities.

In 2002, and again in 2003, Armstrong was named as one of Canada's 50 Best Managed Companies. More than anything this is testament to the progress the corporation has made toward becoming a more highly conductive organization.

The Collaboration Continues

The collaboration between Hubert and Charles further evolved in 2002 when Hubert accepted an invitation to join Armstrong's management board as Executive Vice-President, Strategic Capabilities, with the responsibility for enhancing Armstrong's organizational capabilities and leveraging its e-business platform. Hubert had been involved in Armstrong's strategy session groups since 1998.

Hubert also assumed the role of Co-Chairman at KonvergeandKnow, of which Charles is the founder and chairman. Headquartered in Toronto, KonvergeandKnow develops fully integrated knowledge strategies based on optimized business processes and custom technology solutions. It's the result of a merger between two highly innovative, successful, and complementary companies, one specializing in custom business and technology solutions (Konverge Digital Solutions), the other in knowledge strategy and e-learning platforms (Know Inc).

This book captures the first decade of Hubert's and Charles's relationship, the start of a journey toward building a highly conductive organization.

Acknowledgements

This book reflects experiences from the majority of our working lives—we hesitate to do the calculation of the days, weeks, months, and years that this collectively represents.

Our thinking has been shaped by hundreds of colleagues, practitioners, and researchers, but we'd particularly like to acknowledge the contributions of Karl-Erik Sveiby, Verna Allee, Charles Savage, Leif Edvinsson, Valdis Krebs, Eric Vogt, Masao Maekawa, Dan Sullivan, Brian Hall, Margaret Logan, Barbara Annis, and Pat Sullivan and the ICM Gathering. Having a group of colleagues such as this has enriched our work in countless ways and helped us refine our vision of what a highly conductive organization represents.

We've been fortunate to work in a variety of organizations where we've gained insights from the bumps and bruises along the way while also validating our assumptions in many successful implementations of our ideas. Without the opportunity to put our thinking into practice, our ideas would have remained white-board sketches and sticky note asides. We'd like to acknowledge the staff at Clarica Life Insurance Company and S.A. Armstrong Limited who brought this work to reality—gave it a grounding as well as a workout! In particular, we'd like to acknowledge Bob Astley from Clarica and Jim Armstrong from Armstrong who have given us the encouragement to pursue new ways of doing business, to calibrate our organizations for breakthrough performance.

Creating the book has in itself been a significant learning experience. We've had to sharpen our capabilities, to put our thoughts together in a clear, concise manner, to try to make meaning of the countless bits of information and ideas that we've amassed. The work was truly a collaborative effort with James Creelman, Deb Wallace, Jaylyn Olivo, and Kathy May bringing the project to life. We'd also like to thank our editor, Karen Maloney who patiently guided the development of the central theme.

This book is itself a reflection of a high level of conductivity. With the quality knowledge flow between many thought leaders and practitioners, we've been able to evolve our practice to create a new way of doing business in the knowledge era.

1

The Conductive Organization

On the Move

If it's not shifting paradigms, it's breaking all the rules and understanding that the only constant is change. We're in the midst of a significant transition from all that we once knew about the effective management of organizations to something we understand very little about. The principles and concepts that we've studied, tested, reengineered, and improved upon no longer meet the challenges that current customers bring to the marketplace. With the changes brought by the digital age, globalization, and volatile economies, we're searching for a whole new way of doing business. Practitioners, theorists, business leaders, and academics are all testing the waters, trying to identify the components needed to build an organization that can achieve breakthrough performance in the knowledge era.

We're all a bit puzzled about what's happening. We see very good organizations disappear overnight—what appeared to be a healthy organization just a year ago is now suddenly gone. We believe this is happening, in large part, because organizations aren't staying relevant to their customers. They're not creating and maintaining the right combination of intangible and complementary tangible assets or building the strategic capabilities required to meet their customers' needs.

To succeed, we need to understand the emerging rules of business that will give us a much better lay of the land. Technology is short-circuiting all of the linear ways in which we've organized ourselves. Current business leadership was largely born out of tangible asset management that no longer applies for managing an organization's now more valuable intangible assets. Customers have more choices than ever before and companies have yet to find ways of distinguishing themselves on something other than price and still stay in business.

The key to evolving, to achieving sustainable breakthrough levels of performance year after year, is to sharpen the organizational capabilities needed to meet the challenges of the marketplace. As two practitioners who've had the privilege of leading corporations during the technological, economic, and social change of recent times, we've had the opportunity to apply a number of new approaches and models. We've evolved our thinking and tested our theories in two distinct organizations—Clarica Life Insurance Company (Clarica), a financial services organization, and S. A. Armstrong Limited (Armstrong), an engineering and manufacturing firm. Our positions have enabled us to test the rigor and effectiveness of our approaches in different organizational contexts and marketplaces.

Connectedness

During the past decade, we've seen dramatic disruptions in how societies and organizations are structured. Unparalleled technological advances, in particular the Internet, have led to the dismantling of much of the historically powerful barriers of time and geography. Web-based technologies are connecting people, common interest groups, and organizations in ways that until recently were thought impossible. It's not surprising that two of the most popular websites in the world are currently Ancestry.com and FriendsReunited.com— virtual spaces where people can connect with other people either around the corner or around the globe.

From an organizational perspective, this ability to connect has profound implications for how we structure, manage, lead, and elevate our performance. With billions of bits of data and information being transferred every second of every day, within nations and across continents at the speed of light, a new reality is emerging. Our stakeholders, whether they are shareholders, customers, suppliers, employees, regulatory bodies, or social pressure groups, as well as our competitors have instantaneous access to masses of information about any organization. They have virtually unlimited opportunities to share experiences and to obtain information for making choices.

This new reality is placing enormous strain on organizational leaders in all sectors (e.g., for-profit and not-for-profit, public and private, global and local) to gain and maintain a competitive advantage or high standard of service delivery in a world where the rules we were taught to compete by no longer make sense, or even work.

Risk Management

Just as the field formations and strategies favored by 18th- and 19th-century generals proved to be ineffective and wasteful against 20th-century arsenals, the organizational structures and principles that were once all-powerful and provided security and profit are proving equally ineffective and wasteful within a 21st-century setting. *Fortune Magazine* figures from the 1990s show that only about 30% of organizational strategies were implemented successfully (1), typically leading to the dismissal of even the most charismatic leaders. (We can be thankful that some of the strategies that were developed were NOT implemented. But, we'll come back to strategy later.)

As we move through the next few years, managing the risk of strategic failure will be an even greater priority for executive committees and, in the wake of cataclysmic business failures such as Enron, WorldCom, and others, for their non-executive boards and other shareholder representatives as well. External bodies will increasingly probe corporations for evidence that risk is being managed effectively. They'll be looking for verification that both external risk factors (e.g., regulatory, marketplace, customer, partnerships, reputation) and internal risk factors (e.g., accounting and behavioral transparency, talent management, organizational structures, systems) are being judiciously managed.

An Opportunity for Leaders

Leaders who find effective ways to detect, mitigate, and act upon these many pressure points will be well placed to gain competitive advantage for their organizations going forward. In a broader sense, they'll also be playing an important historic role as they take organizations to their next evolutionary stage of organizing structures and principles—a stage that is knowledge based rather than industrially based and intangibly rather than tangibly driven.

Being organizational leaders at this time in history presents us with an exciting opportunity to reconsider the old paradigms that we were taught were the building blocks of good management and good organizational design. We have the challenge of figuring out what a knowledge-era organization looks like and what makes it tick. In doing so, we'll experiment with many new approaches. Most likely our designs will be made up of bits and pieces from our trial and error attempts—we'll learn from experience what works and what doesn't.

The Beginning of a Conversation

Although this book describes the components we've found valuable in the configuration of knowledge-era, connected organizations, we don't suggest that these elements will go unchallenged. Rather, we offer them with the expectation that they'll start a conversation among executives, managers, and practitioners who will lead corporations toward sustainable high performance. We offer to the emerging body of thinking a starting point for discussion and experimentation, not a definitive description with a prescriptive guide on how to get there. Our belief is that no single organization is capable of working out this complex challenge on its own. We need to collaborate, to contribute our collective experiences and ideas to an ongoing conversation. We need one another's perspectives to develop a full picture of what's emerging.

The tools, techniques, and approaches that we outline and the language we use transcend traditional organizational boundaries. They are as applicable internally as they are externally. This new extended dynamic meshes the external with the internal and offers leaders and practitioners a new perspective on managing organizations and mitigating some of the risk they face in a connected world.

The Conductive Organization

As with any new thinking, we find it useful to focus our ideas through a central, unifying image that captures and reflects our ideas, concepts, and models. For us, an apt image for successful organizations in the knowledge era is the ***conductive organization***.

Borrowing from the laws of science and applying them to the art of business, we define the conductive organization as:

An organization that continuously generates and renews capabilities to achieve breakthrough performance by enhancing the quality and flow of knowledge and by calibrating its strategy, culture, structure, and systems to the needs of its customers and the marketplace.

This definition highlights the key dimensions and organizational capabilities that create the framework for our ideas. It outlines the components that we believe need to be in place for an organization to be viable in the knowledge era. We need to:

- Continuously generate capabilities
- Increase the quality and speed at which knowledge flows within the organization and with and between our customers and employees
- Synchronize our key organizational capabilities
- Calibrate our organizing structures and principles to our customers and marketplace.

Core Organizational Capabilities in the Conductive Organization

The knowledge era, digital age, networked economy, or any one of the new labels given to this all-encompassing change in our lives demands that we rethink the way we design and operate our organizations and interact with our customers. Our belief is that we do have the capabilities to meet these challenges by assembling five core components. These integral organizational capabilities provide a framework to organize our collective experience through a discussion of strategy, culture, structure, systems, and leadership (see Figure 1.1). Working in strategic symmetry, fed by a highly conductive, quality knowledge flow, these capabilities form the building blocks of the conductive organization.

Strategy

The first and foundational core organizational capability is strategy. Achieving breakthrough performance depends, in large part, on the extent to which the strategies and the business activities that flow

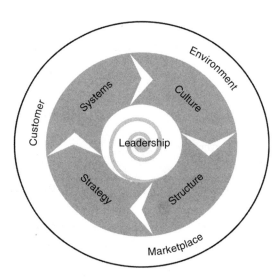

Figure 1.1 Core Organizational Capabilities Model for the Conductive Organization

from these strategies are responding to what's actually happening in the marketplace.

Strategy vs. Strategy Making

The conductive organization makes a distinction between strategy and strategy making. A strategy is an objective, something you arrive at, a conclusion. Strategy making is an action, a process that you follow, a capability. When we talk about strategy as an organizational capability, we are really talking about strategy making—*the constant renewal of strategy to align and keep pace with the evolution of customer and marketplace needs.*

Strategy making in many cases expands the organization's strategic horizon. It uncovers new customer needs and opens up opportunities that the organization can explore. Generating the capabilities needed to realize recalibrated strategies becomes a new constant that keeps the customer at the center of the organization.

Organization Strategies and Knowledge Strategies

None of what we describe in this chapter and throughout the book can be implemented without a well-honed organization strategy with an embedded knowledge strategy. These strategies form the road map for the transformation to a higher state of conductivity. Although the eventual goal may be that knowledge strategies are absorbed into business strategies and the strategy-making process, in the beginning it's important to articulate a specific knowledge strategy. Knowledge strategies provide the framework for eliminating the obstacles and resistance to knowledge flow and capability generation.

Culture

The second core organizational capability of the highly conductive organization is culture. An organization's culture reflects the collective mindsets of its employees. It's best represented by, "That's just how things are done around here." Organizational cultures need to be constantly renewed to keep relevant to the marketplace. The best way to accelerate the evolution of a culture is to:

- Build on values that are already collectively held by individuals
- Insert new values that are complementary to existing values and that correspond to the organization's strategic aspirations
- Understand what customers value
- Create alignment with customer expectations.

By systematically unearthing employee values, an organization's culture can be identified, harnessed, and shaped, becoming an integral organizational capability for enabling high-quality performance.

Structure

To support the transition, an organization needs to group its employees and their responsibilities into new roles and suggest how relationships between new structures can be integrated to form a whole. To enable an unimpeded flow of quality knowledge at an accelerated pace, we need to rethink traditional organizational structures and create new groupings that are aligned to our strategy and to our capability to calibrate to customer needs.

This calibration requires new capabilities that are applied externally as well as practiced internally. If high-trust relationships, partnering mindsets, and meaningful conversations are all qualities that we expect to exhibit with our customers and value-creation network partners, then we must have structures that are aligned to support the internal practice of these qualities.

Systems

The fourth core organizational capability in the conductive organization is systems—the assembly of all horizontal and vertical processes across the organization that enable it to implement its strategy. We use the term *system* to mean a connected arrangement of elements that make a whole. Its use is compared with physical systems like the solar system or an ecosystem, or in the context of the human body, the circulatory system or nervous system. The use of systems in an organizational context is not limited to a focus on computer systems.

An organization is a complex collection of many different systems that, for example, track finances, develop new products, deliver customer service, and support the technology infrastructure. All of these systems work in concert to accomplish the organization's strategy, meet stakeholder expectations, and deliver products and services to customers.

Leadership

Leadership sits at the center of the organizational capability model for the conductive organization. It triggers the organizational dynamic, creating the tensions needed to keep the other four key organizational capabilities calibrated to the customer. It synchronizes strategy, systems, structure, and culture—keeps them evolving to meet changing customer requirements. Leadership mobilizes and determines the quality and rate of knowledge flow, providing a catalyst for others to exercise their responsibilities, encouraging self-initiation, trust, interdependence, and partnering across the organization.

We define leadership as *the manner in which individuals choose to exercise their responsibilities.* We purposely use individuals and not managers because we see leadership as a capability that must be encouraged and nurtured within all employees, not just the few who sit at the top of the organizational chart. However, we also recognize that employees have varying degrees of leadership accountabilities. And that while everyone in the organization is encouraged to exercise their leadership capabilities in appropriate ways as dictated by customer needs, leadership at the senior and managerial levels has added accountabilities to set direction, manage performance, and make decisions that affect the dynamics of the organization.

Leadership is an organizational capability. While individuals develop capabilities to better exercise their leadership, the organization creates the context for leadership. We've all seen instances where people with highly developed leadership skills can't exercise their leadership to its fullest in an unsupportive organizational context. On the other hand, the right leadership context will elevate everyone's ability to exercise leadership—not just in managerial levels.

Dimensions of the Conductive Organization

To identify the many dimensions of a conductive organization, we began by listing its characteristics—its symptomatic behaviors and distinguishing features. We then moved to focusing on performance (the outcomes, the ends) and the approaches (the processes, the means) for achieving goals. Our conclusion is that the highly conductive organization seems to be one that always gets it right, that is always on the mark—that doesn't ever seem to miss the point. The analysis of its dimensions is slightly more complicated, as you no doubt expected. If it were easy, we'd have all figured it out by now and be ready to move on to the next challenge.

A highly conductive organization is a complex system of interdependent components. The dimensions that we've identified include:

More aware of customer needs and marketplace changes. A highly conductive organization has moved beyond the notion of customer-focused or customer-centric. It has, as John Seeley Brown described, undertaken a "regrinding of its lenses"—formulated a new way of looking at the world through the eyes of the customer. This repositioning of thinking, of viewing the total landscape through the customer's perspective, means that the organization now interprets its own environment based on how its customers see things. It looks at everything from its customers' perspective—from the outside in—to take into account its competitors' behavior, environmental factors, supplier issues, its customers' customers, and their own capabilities. The conductive organization works *back* from the customer.

The conductive nature of the organization is based on its ability to constantly seek out what's happening with the customer—to bring that reality, the customer's reality, *into* the organization and then respond to that evolving reality on a real-time basis. The customer perspective focuses the energies of the organization. There are no wasted resources spent on solutions that we *think* the customer needs. Through a deep understanding of the customer, we know what we need to achieve for the customer, and we can structure and develop our organization to meet those needs.

Customer-calibrated. A key proposition for the highly conductive organization is that it gears its own development to what it wants to achieve with its customers. The customer sits in the middle of everything the organization does. The organization wraps itself around its customers, calibrates, and then continuously recalibrates its strategy, systems, structure, and culture to align with customer needs as they evolve. It uses the outside-in perspective to guide its choices.

Identifying the customer's environment, looking at the world through the customer's eyes is only one part of the process. The knowledge gained from external conversations has to be brought inside the organization to make meaning of what is being sensed. The organization needs to put this knowledge into the wider perspective of the whole marketplace and understand what it means in terms of its capabilities and what it needs to do to react—to take action in determining how the organization is going to go about serving its customers and the marketplace.

Balanced horizontal and vertical structure. To meet customer needs, to successfully implement customer-calibrated strategies, the conductive organization builds an internal organizing structure that works as well horizontally across the organization as it does through its vertical hierarchy. It has highly developed collaborative capabilities that support the formation, disbanding, and reformation of cross-functional teams that bring their combined expertise to the table to design solutions and solve customer problems.

The traditional vertical axis of work (i.e., I'm the boss. I ask you to do something. You do it within your functional unit.) is counterbalanced with work accomplished across silos. The conductive organization has as much horizontal life, energy, and intensity for achieving breakthrough performance as it does vertically. By putting the customer at the center of the organization, cross-functional value-adding processes can become more highly developed.

Constructive context for leadership. The highly conductive organization not only builds leadership capabilities in its employees, it creates an environment in which leaders can flourish. It has defined leadership principles, articulated the role of leadership in the organization, and created a trusting environment where all individuals can exercise their leadership to the fullest extent. Encouraging self-initiation, innovation, and collaboration, the leadership context supports individuals at all levels of the organization to exercise their responsibilities and uphold their commitment to create value for customers.

High-quality relationships. Relationships are the conduits for conversations that support knowledge flow. They're the vehicles by which trust is established and maintained. They connect the organization, its customers, and employees. They form the foundation for collaboration as a way of generating new capabilities and collectively finding innovative solutions. These high-quality relationships are made possible through the adoption of core values.

In order to create high-quality relationships, the organization must first practice the necessary skills internally before they can be applied externally. They must develop high-quality interpersonal skills and partnering mindsets that instill trust and a will to collaborate. Only an organization that collaborates effectively internally can collaborate effectively externally. External partnerships are severely limited by an internal climate that makes it difficult to work horizontally across the organization.

Coherence in business processes. Coherence is created when business processes—the approaches used to enable employees to achieve business objectives—are aligned with the brand promise and core values. How the organization accomplishes its goals needs to be consonant with the organization's character (expressed internally and externally through the brand promise) and the core values that guide its behavior. Coherence exists when there's integrity between what an organization says and what it does or how it acts.

Clear brand promise. The brand is a qualitative reflection of the organization's character that is aligned with core values. It's a way of projecting a desired image that can be verified through experiencing the brand promise. It's an internal as well as external expression—employees commit to live the brand promise internally as they deliver the same promise externally. The brand is a mechanism for facilitating new conversations with customers and employees. It's a statement about the kind of relationship the organization wants to develop and grow—a way of communicating the expected experience people will have with the organization. The brand and core values that support it are key tools for bringing coherence to the organization.

Leveraged technology platform. A comprehensive technology infrastructure is a system that a highly conductive organization leverages to enable collaboration and learning. It's seamlessly integrated into work processes, geared to people's needs for accomplishing their objectives. It facilitates conversations, access to information, knowledge sharing—all at the convenience of its users. It manages the organization's knowledge assets—accumulating, storing, and preserving for ready access by anyone who might need them.

Employees and customers have the capabilities to leverage the technology platform. They're skilled in software functionality and information retrieval. They utilize the technology for just-in-time learning, collaborating virtually and increasing process efficiencies.

Knowledge Strategy. To evolve from its current state to a highly conductive state, an organization needs a knowledge strategy embedded in its larger organization strategy that outlines the core capabilities needed to meet its strategic intent. Like self-dissolving stitches or time-released medication, the knowledge strategy, over time, becomes assimilated. As its transformational knowledge principles and concepts become *just the way we do our work around here*, the need for a separate strategy is subsumed.

The knowledge strategy focuses the organization's energies on creating the capabilities to meet customer requirements and expands the organization's strategic horizon. Using its knowledge strategy as its guide, a highly conductive organization successfully applies a higher level of quality and broad-based harnessing of all resources at its disposal.

Capabilities match need. The capabilities that the organization needs to meet customer requirements are generated in a systematic, purposeful way. Learning, collaborating, and strategy making are accomplished in real time at a speed that is equal to the pace of changing customer needs. As a result, the highly conductive organization has the right configuration of capabilities in the right place at the right time to take advantage of opportunities as they present themselves.

Strategic capabilities. These capabilities, both individual and organizational, are elevated to a *strategic* level because they are specifically needed to realize the organization's strategy. They are often capabilities that will distinguish an organization in its marketplaces. Strategic capabilities evolve over time in an organization and may even go unnoticed or unarticulated until they are developed to such a degree that they become obvious embedded capabilities. In other instances, strategic capabilities have been articulated as being required to meet evolving customer needs and are linked with the strategic imperatives included in all levels of strategy—business, customer, organization, and knowledge.

Strategic symmetry. To evolve from its current state to a highly conductive state, the organization must ensure that there is a symmetry among its business strategy, customer strategy, organization strategy, and knowledge strategy. Of these four strategic focuses, the overarching business strategy calibrates to the customer strategy and its environment. The organizational strategy, with its embedded knowledge strategy, addresses the capabilities and mechanisms required to bring the overarching business strategy to life in service of the customer.

These strategies are symmetrical and connected—they embody one another and enable each other. As they build in concert with one another, the organization systematically increases its reach into the marketplace and outdistances its competitors.

Sustainable breakthrough performance. Our definition of a conductive organization is anchored in performance. In fact, it's all about performance—that's why we're doing what we're doing. Performance gives us the freedom to be who we want to be. But with that freedom comes the responsibility of finding the right combination of components to make the organization work, the right approaches to achieve desired outcomes.

There's a clear distinction between performance and *sustainable* performance. The perspective we present is one not only of short-term financial, market-centric performance but one that includes a healthy view of the organization's strategic horizon—the possibilities the organization is open to. An organization that secures sustainable performance builds a foundation to help it continue operating at an optimal level, the ability to constantly recalibrate to meet new opportunities presented by the customer and marketplace.

Performance isn't just about the bottom line. How this performance is generated becomes a key factor in the organization's ability to constantly surpass itself by breaking through self-imposed performance patterns.

Our goal is to achieve *breakthrough* performance—aspiring to what may well be the impossible. With the capabilities needed in place, in an integrated, mutually reinforcing, and cohesive fashion, the organization can break through existing patterns and trends.

To summarize these 12 dimensions of a highly conductive organization, we've compiled the key points, looking first at the end (the performance outcome) and then the means (the process of getting there).

Table 1.1 Dimensions of a Conductive Organization

End or Outcome	Means or Process
Customer focus. More aware of customer needs/preferences and sensitive to market changes/shifts	Takes an outside-in and inside-out perspective
Customer-calibrated. Customer strategies driven by knowledge of customer and marketplace	Places the customer in the center of capability and strategy development Ability to sense and respond
Balanced organizational structure. Works vertically as well as horizontally	Works through cross-functional, value adding processes
Environment. Has cohesive culture, systems, structures, and strategies that support a constructive context for leadership	Creates and fosters an environment where individuals can exercise their leadership to the fullest extent
Relationships. High-quality relationships both internally and externally	Develops high-quality interpersonal skills and partnering mindsets; instills trust and a will to collaborate
Coherence. High degree of coherence in business approaches —how you do business	Leverages corporate values
Brand. Realization of the brand promise	Lives the brand promise internally and externally
Technology. Leveraged technology platform/infrastructure	Creates a platform that is embedded in the way people work
Knowledge strategy. Continuous renewal of capabilities at individual and organizational levels	Participates in a continuous strategy-making process addressing the creation, management, and use of knowledge
Aligned capabilities. Capabilities match fast-evolving needs of customers	Capabilities are enhanced as an inherent part of resolving issues and meeting challenges
Strategic capabilities. Supportive of strategic intent.	Identifies the capabilities needed to distinguish the organization in its marketplace
Strategic symmetry. Cohesive realization of strategies	Able to renew capabilities in parallel to business strategy
Performance. Breakthrough, sustainable performance	Evolves toward conductive state, leveraging strategy, systems, culture, and structure to break through to new levels of performance

These dimensions are further developed throughout the book in illustrations of the principles and concepts, tools and approaches, and desired outcomes of the conductive organization. Some of these dimensions represent new vocabulary that is defined in greater detail within the context of the frameworks, processes, and tools that we use to describe our experience with new organizing structures and principles. A glossary at the end of the book may also prove to be useful for clarifying meaning.

Key Concepts

Before we go much further, it's important to understand two key concepts that are fundamental to our thinking about how to build a highly conductive organization: *capabilities* and *conductivity*.

Capabilities

More than abilities, competencies, or resources, capabilities represent *a collection of cross-functional elements that come together to create the potential for taking effective action.* These elements include: attributes, skills, knowledge, systems, and structures. Capabilities represent tangible and intangible components that are needed to enable performance. Simply, capabilities are the link between strategy and performance (see Figure 1.2).

While there are a number of different types of capabilities, we talk about three types in some depth when we describe the components of a highly conductive organization: *organizational* capabilities, *individual* capabilities, and *generative* capabilities.

Organizational Capabilities. An organization is a complex collection of components working in dynamic relationships to create a whole. Organizational capabilities refer to the *know-how* of the organization—the frameworks and platforms that support the ability of individuals to work effectively to make the organization a successful enterprise. Organizational capabilities include *the strategies, systems, structures, culture, and leadership that make up an organiza-*

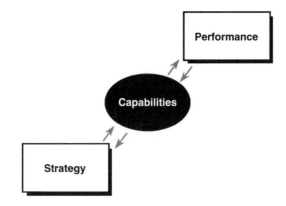

Figure 1.2 Capabilities—Link between Strategy and Performance

tion. These are the five key organizational capabilities that we focus on as the building blocks of the conductive organization.

Individual Capabilities. Individuals, like organizations, have a variety of capabilities that enable them to achieve their objectives for creating value for the customer. They're a combination of the observable employee-applied knowledge, skills, and behavior in the workplace and the attitudes and values that guide that behavior. The capabilities of an individual are composed of *his/her attributes, competencies, mindsets, and values.*

Because we've targeted our discussion at the organizational level, we don't spend much time talking about capabilities from the perspective of the individual employee. But there's a parallel need to generate individual capabilities in order for many of the organizational capabilities we outline to be generated. Culture (organizational) and mindsets (individual) are the linking points between the two types of capabilities (see Figure 1.3).

The organization's culture needs to reflect the collectively held values of its individual employees. The best way to unlock a culture and accelerate its evolution is to address the alignment between individual and organizational values.

Generative Capabilities. The ability to continuously generate new capabilities is crucial for the organization to evolve at the speed

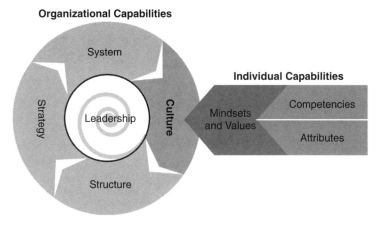

Figure 1.3 Individual and Organizational Capabilities

of market change. We create new and improve existing capabilities at both the organizational and individual level through *generative capabilities*. Knowledge flows feed generative capabilities that we've defined as *capabilities that enable the continuous generation of other capabilities*. Three key generative capabilities are highly developed in a conductive organization: learning, collaborating, and strategy making.

Conductivity

One of the mostly highly developed qualities in the conductive organization is *conductivity*. It's the distinguishing characteristic in the knowledge era that is fundamental to achieving breakthrough performance. Throughout our discussion of ideas, conductivity is a central theme. We define it as *the capability to effectively transmit high-quality knowledge throughout the organization as well as with and between customers and employees*.

Like a vector, which has both substance and direction, conductivity has a dimension of quality in addition to the speed of transmission, a filtering to ensure that only relevant, validated information and knowledge are transmitted.

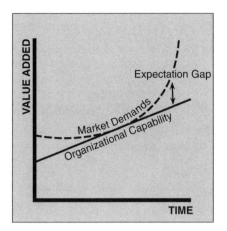 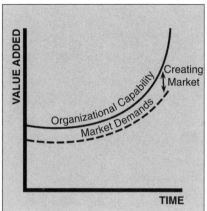

Figure 1.4   Market Demands

The concept of conductivity is based on building the generative capabilities required to turn information into knowledge that can be acted upon to create value for the customer and the organization. The level of conductivity within an organization improves by a purposeful, systematic approach to enabling reliable knowledge flows that support the organization in generating relevant capabilities at the speed that evolving customer needs demand.

A high level of conductivity ensures that the organization is closely linked to its customers and the marketplace so that it can develop products and services based on a sense-and-respond mode as opposed to the traditional make-and-sell mode of the industrial era (see Figure 1.4).

In all marketplaces, customers are increasingly more demanding of how they want their needs and expectations met. In response, organizations are developing solutions and services that are more highly customized, integrated, and complex. If they don't keep up with the exponentially rising demands, a gap is created and the market continues to out-distance the organization. Within a short period of time, the organization is no longer relevant and is in danger of ceasing to exist.

The ability to develop the capabilities required to introduce new solutions at a pace that meets the rapidly evolving needs of customers and outdistances competitors results in breakthrough performance for the highly conductive organization.

Conclusion

Just as our organizations face the challenge of operating in a new, more complex, and highly interconnected environment with historical practices, so do we face similar hurdles in using the linear, two-dimensional technology of writing on paper to describe the complex interdependencies of this evolving perspective on an organization's performance.

We believe that performance can be enhanced through the systematic design of new ways of doing business. Our experiences in bringing organizations to higher states of conductivity are filled with exciting challenges that have tested our vision and stretched our own individual capabilities.

What seems an impossible task can be achieved through the systematic design of new ways of doing business. With new concepts, new language, and a new focus on core organizational capabilities, we have the opportunity to build organizations that are highly conductive and calibrated to the customer in order to achieve breakthrough performance.

Emerging Principles

- New technologies impacting on human communication drive new organizing principles and structures.

- Technology is short-circuiting all the linear ways in which we've structured our organizations.

- A highly conductive organization has formulated a new way of looking at the world through the eyes of the customer.

- Strategy making is an activity that improves as the organizational membrane becomes more porous so that everyone relates to achieving an elevated customer experience.

- A new order of risk is associated with increased reliance on intangible assets—it's more complex, difficult to detect, and lethal if ignored.

- High-quality relationships support core values.

- The organization must learn to partner internally before it can partner externally.

- The brand is a qualitative reflection of the organization's character as expressed by its core values.

- Performance gives freedom to be who we want to be, to express our collective greatness as individuals, to actualize our full potential, and to realize our destiny.

- Three generative capabilities in a highly conductive organization are learning, collaborating, and strategy making. These capabilities give the organization the inherent ability to renew itself as it encounters new challenges.

- Strategy making is an action verb as opposed to a noun or an object. It's an embedded process as opposed to a finite set of activities in a defined time cycle. It's a key capability geared to ensure constant renewal—creating relevance in the marketplace.

Reference

1. Charan, R. "Why CEOs Fail." *Fortune Magazine.* (June 21, 1999).

2

The Customer Imperative

Introduction

Central to the highly conductive organization is a continuous flow of knowledge from the customer to the organization, where strategy, culture, structures, and systems are all calibrated to customer needs. The purpose of creating an organization capable of unimpeded knowledge flow and continuous learning is to build value at the customer interface. In order for these flows to create value for the customer, knowledge has to be transmitted freely throughout the organization and employees must take an outside-in perspective. As a result of this conductivity, new capabilities are created for customers, the organization, and its employees. High-performing organizations know how to build and maintain the relationships that are the conduits for knowledge flow, leveraging capabilities and strategy-making processes.

The customer is at the core of everything an organization does. With the current rate of accelerated change, where uncertainty and ambiguity are the only constants, the most effective way an organization can function is to be totally wired, totally connected to its customers. We need a high-quality and timely flow of knowledge that leads to action that in turn creates value for the customer and the organization. Understanding the customer imperative and calibrating the organization to customer needs is what will make breakthrough performance possible in the knowledge era.

Beyond Established Notions

From our perspective, the customer imperative requires that we go beyond established notions of customer focus or customer-centricity. It's more than customer service or product quality. It touches on more than the one or two departments with direct customer contact responsibility and encompasses more than targeted, one-time, or episodic change programs. The new customer imperative requires a systematic and continuous alignment and realignment of capabilities throughout the organization. We need the agility to adapt to slight changes in customer requirements or more seismic shifts in customers' directions.

Although much of the literature and thinking in the last decade about putting the customer first has been useful and has certainly influenced our thinking, most leaders will honestly admit to being farther than ever from keeping pace with exponentially rising customer demands. By some order of magnitude, it is still the greatest challenge we face both operationally and strategically. We all risk strategic and operational failure as a result of organizational misalignment with the customer.

Mitigating this risk requires that we challenge the mental constructs through which we think about, relate to, and respond to customers.

New Customer Standards

Customers' expectations are increasingly driven by how they experience product or service offerings in other spheres of their lives. Their expectations are formed, not just by their use of products or services in their workplace, but in every aspect of their lives.

For example, if people can go online, book an airline ticket, choose their seats, and make special meal requests with the click of a mouse, they'll use this experience as the benchmark for the flexibility and speed they expect from all organizations that supply them with goods or services. Individual industries or sectors are no longer setting the bar for their own service quality levels.

The implications of this new customer reality are far-reaching and will certainly contribute to the gap between market demands and organizational capabilities that we discussed in chapter 1 (see Figure 1.3). Closing this gap requires multidimensional interventions. But from a simple, practical customer-facing viewpoint, we need to challenge our conventional notions of customer satisfaction and loyalty.

Customer Satisfaction and Loyalty

It's too easy for us to view customer-facing performance relative to our competitors and to judge customer satisfaction and potential customer loyalty on the basis of that relative position. If the customer gives an 80% satisfaction rate to one supplier and 70% to another, the organization that received the 80% rating may assume it's largely assured the customer's business and loyalty. There's no question that we all strive to satisfy our customers. But given the bewildering range of products and services customers can choose from and the opportunities for new competitors even from unexpected sources (e.g., supermarkets offering financial services—loans and mortgages), relying on customer satisfaction figures alone is more than likely a misguided strategy.

Measures of loyalty may be of little more use than customer satisfaction ratings. Customers may show loyalty for no other reason than the fact that there is, at the time, no clearly superior supplier— a situation that can change in an instant with new competitors entering the marketplace. Alternatively, loyalty may be a result of the customer's not yet taking the time to switch suppliers—something that is common in the financial services industry. A targeted campaign by a competitor can easily turn the customer's head.

Measures of satisfaction and loyalty typically convince organizational leaders that they own these customers, in keeping with industrial-era thinking about suppliers shaping and controlling their markets. Today, owning a customer is neither a reasonable aspiration nor a sensible one. Customers will, and should, go where they perceive the greatest value as they define it.

A New Customer Language

From our experience, abandoning or at least revising established ideas of customer loyalty and satisfaction requires the scripting of a new customer-facing language, a language that more accurately describes the value the customer derives from its relationship with an organization and the value the organization derives from its relationship with the customer. This language has less to do with satisfaction and loyalty and more to do with *generalized reciprocity.*

Generalized reciprocity is a state in which all parties (e.g., suppliers, customers, partners, employees) contribute something of value to the relationship and all parties also derive value from that relationship. The result is a desire by everyone to continue the relationship. We've found generalized reciprocity to be a much more powerful measure of sustainable success than static measures of customer satisfaction or loyalty.

Within our exploration of shaping a new customer-facing language, we've started from the premise that customers today are looking for a relationship with their suppliers that is solution rather than product based. The question we've posed for ourselves is less "what product can we provide?" and more "what problem is the customer grappling with?" or "what aspiration will this solution help the customer achieve?"

Trust-Based Relationships

In working with customers to identify solutions, we find that they'll typically only enter long-term relationships that are built on trust. Trust between parties is a prerequisite for generalized reciprocity, the two-way knowledge flow that is the basis for conductivity. Customers want to trust that the supplier is looking to deliver long-term value rather than a quick sale. At the same time, the supplier needs to trust that the customer is providing accurate information and is a willing partner in the development of a solution.

We've found it useful to recognize that through this trust customers are looking to shape each transaction or solution to their needs. Quite simply, customers want to feel in control of what they are doing. They want to feel that they are making their own choices and not having choices foisted on them by a supplier. This scenario represents a significant power shift from the industrial era, when the predominant attitude was "if we make it, the customer will buy it." To meet the customers' need for control of choice, a highly conductive organization has shifted from a product-based to a relationship-based solution. Table 2.1 outlines the core differences between these two orientations.

Customer Values

Within the knowledge-era customer/supplier dynamic, customers are more likely to enter relationships with, and purchase from, suppliers who have characteristics and values similar to their own. If customers value protecting the environment, they will naturally gravitate toward suppliers they believe are equally environmentally conscious and will abandon suppliers they believe are not.

The classic case is the original Body Shop who recognized that, by selling cosmetics that weren't tested on animals and were environmentally friendly, they could attract customers from other cosmetic suppliers. They believed that many cosmetics users shared these values and would have no compunction about dropping their present suppliers—no matter how satisfied they were with their current suppliers' products. This assumption proved true. Body Shop helped their customers realize their aspiration of living up to their values of caring for the environment and the welfare of animals.

Table 2.1 Product vs. Relationship Solution Orientations

	Product Orientation	Relationship Solution Orientation
Strategy	Based on number of products sold, market share, and product-based profitability	Based on number of customers reached, share of wallet, and customer profitability
Format	Standardized items aimed at broadly defined customer segments	Individualized combinations of product/information/service
Integration	Customer's operations adjusted to meet product integration	Solution configured to readily fit into the customer's environment
Price	Commodity approach. Sold at fixed prices based on production costs plus margin	Value-based approach. Price based on value realized by the customer that is attributed to the solution

Just Ahead of the Customer

For the conductive organization, customer calibration is not just about reacting to changing market or customer demands. It means being *market makers.* These organizations know their customers so well that they can develop a solution that provides great value to customers before customers recognize that they actually require it.

The objective is to be calibrated so you are just ahead of the customer, essentially occupying the next natural place for the customer to go. We emphasize *just* ahead as an important qualifier. There's little value in being so far ahead of the customer that you create solutions that customers won't actually want for many years—there's no value in outpacing the customer. A conductive organization possesses the ability to generate capabilities at the speed that the market *requires* them.

A classic example is the creation of the minivan at Chrysler. Before the concept of a minivan was developed, Chrysler held focus groups with potential customers. When asked what type of vehicle they needed, participants stated that they required something that was easily accessible and had lots of room to carry groceries and other parcels—something to support the lifestyle of a suburban family. No one specifically asked for a minivan—in fact it hadn't even been conceptualized at this point. Instead, Chrysler listened to their marketplace and developed a vehicle design specifically calibrated to customer needs.

There are many more examples of organizations that have been able to place themselves just ahead of the customer and have reaped the substantial financial benefits of doing so. Conversely, there are numerous examples of corporations launching products onto the market that, however clever, were not what the market wanted at the time.

The Chrysler minivan example demonstrates how new product development and introduction can be solution as opposed to product driven. The customer wanted an integrated solution to accessibility/space problems, not just an enhancement of an existing car, which had been the subject of discussion.

Creating a Sense-and-Respond Capability

Creating the minivan is a good illustration of taking a sense-and-respond rather than a make-and-sell approach to providing solutions for customers. With a sense-and-respond mindset, the organization can detect, in near real time, what's happening in their marketplace and deploy immediate responsive strategies. The capability to operate in a sense-and-respond mode is a key dimension of the highly conductive organization. It is systemic and impacts every fiber of the organization. It necessitates full knowledge of how both the organization and the customer behave and interact, as well as where value is created.

To understand the position from which a sense-and-respond organization competes, we turn to work completed by Goldman, Nagel and Preiss (1) on served and unserved markets (see Figure 2.1). The bottom left quadrant represents how customers are being

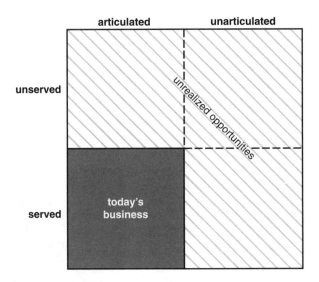

Figure 2.1 Serving Customer Needs

served today—where products and services are presently offered in the marketplace. The customer has articulated a need and a solution has been provided. The bottom right quadrant is the potential for unrealized value from a customer who is receiving value but being requested to pay for it. This value, which more than likely is intangible, has the potential to generate a revenue stream—it just hasn't been articulated as of yet even though it's already being served.

The top left quadrant represents the articulated requirement of customers who aren't being fully served, but whose needs are known. The top right quadrant is the unarticulated requirements of customers. By uncovering these unarticulated needs and being first to market with solutions (i.e., moving into the bottom right quadrant), the conductive organization can secure a significant competitive advantage. It's possible to compete from the bottom left to bottom right quadrants, but competition is fierce and margins often prove difficult to maintain at any reasonable level. The greatest competitive advantage is to uncover the unarticulated needs of the customer and become the first market mover.

First-Mover Advantage

Competing from the top right quadrant (unarticulated need, unserved market) requires a high level of conductivity within the organization. It's a challenging place to reach, but when organizations get there, they can claim what we describe as *first-mover advantage*. An organization with first-mover advantage is so well calibrated to the needs of its customers that it leads the market on the basis of its own strengths—the capabilities that it has generated in real time by learning with the customer. It forces competitors into a position of being followers and of having to compete on the basis of their weaknesses.

Goldman, Nagel, and Preiss working in the Agility Forum (1) from the Iacocca Institute at Lehigh University in Pennsylvania developed the concept of *the window of business opportunity*. This illustration offers evidence of the potential financial payback of first-mover advantage. The window refers to the period during which a business proposition has relevance in the marketplace. According to this theory, 80% of the available profits from any opportunity are harvested in the first half of the window.

For example, a new laptop computer is relevant in the marketplace for about seven months. So, 80% of the profits are realized within the first 3.5 months of its introduction. If a laptop supplier is not in the marketplace competing within the first window, little profit is left—and little, if any, competitive advantage can be gained from its efforts to enter this marketplace.

What the window of opportunity illustrates is that organizations that are first to market with required customer solutions will reap the lion's share of the profits. Their competitors are left to fight for scraps—and very little margin. We add that only a highly conductive organization will have the capabilities to operate in the first part of the window.

In many markets, the window of opportunity narrows as competition intensifies. As a result, organizations are increasingly placed under severe pressure to identify the new customer-facing solutions that will result in first-mover advantage. The conductive organization is configured and able to recalibrate to make first-mover advantage not just an aspiration, but a distinctive capability. The pivot point of the organization's customer interactions should be the speed and quality of knowledge flow—a high degree of conductivity.

Innovation

Quality knowledge flows, strong trusting relationships, and generative capabilities enable organizations and their customers to learn from one another with each business transaction. Knowledge, therefore, serves as the platform for constant innovation and evolution of the solutions that take customers to the next place they want to be.

Innovation requires that organizations create and maintain solution-based relationships that demand a high degree of involvement with the customer. If the customer is actively involved in, learning with, and gaining value from this relationship, then it's much more likely that the relationship will be sustainable over time.

Value Creation Networked Solutions

Delivering to ever-expanding customer requirements has led to an explosive growth in partners working together to craft customer-centric solutions. In this new networked model, partners (who may compete in other areas of the marketplace) join to contribute their own capabilities to the value creation process. We'll discuss this concept in more depth in later chapters, but the customer plays an important role and the need for conductivity is even greater in this new structure for designing and delivering customer solutions.

Participating in a value creation network is an increasingly strong motivator for accessing required capabilities. One organization may not possess the capabilities it requires to meet the customer's need, and it may be largely incapable of creating that capability in the time frame necessary to realize first-mover advantage. For example, the capability may be too expensive or too time intensive to generate.

As a result, the drive to take advantage of the 80% of profits from the first half of the window of opportunity is leading to increased strategic alliances between organizations, as they recognize that it is better to share 80% of the profits with a competitor than to enter the marketplace in the second half of the window.

A highly conductive organization is more capable of successfully participating in one of these value creation networks because, once again, the customer imperative is foremost in its strategy. While a great deal of energy is required to sustain these networks, the organization must not lose sight of its customer in the process of managing its relationships with the other network partners.

Conclusion

The customer imperative is driving the need for highly conductive organizations. Without the customer fully at the center of all aspects of the organization, the organization will not be able to achieve breakthrough performance with first-mover advantage. Key to understanding the customer imperative is recognizing the importance of establishing high-trust relationships that enable knowledge flow and engage the customer in jointly developing innovative solutions. Without adopting this new perspective, organizations in the knowledge era will lose their relevance and, over time, if not in short order, will cease to be viable.

In the next two chapters, we talk more about the central role of customers in the context of customer capital (one of the three components of our Knowledge Capital Model) and the art of customer calibration.

Emerging Principles

- One of the greatest risks an organization can face is to become misaligned with the customer at the operational and strategic levels.

- Breakthrough performance is improbable without developing frequent and close customer calibration as a distinctive capability.

- Owning the customer is neither a reasonable aspiration nor a sensible one.

- The conductive organization can generate capabilities at the speed the market requires them.

- First-mover advantage evolves from real-time learning with the customer.

- Customers are looking to shape solutions and transactions specifically to fit their needs. They want their preferences remembered with each transaction.

- An organization with first-mover advantage is so well calibrated to the needs of its customers that it shapes the market based on its strengths—the capabilities that it has generated in real time by learning with the customer.

- High-performing organizations know how to build and maintain the relationships that are the conduits for knowledge flow, leveraging capabilities and strategy-making processes.

- The new customer imperative requires a systematic and continuous alignment and realignment of capabilities throughout the organization.

Reference

1. For information on the Agility Forum, see *http://www.iacocca-lehigh.org* and Goldman, S.L., R.N. Nagel, and K. Preiss (1995). *Agile Competitors and Virtual Organizations: Strategies for Enriching the Customer*. New York: Van Nostrand Reinhold.

3

The Knowledge Capital Model

Introduction

In order to remain viable, an organization has to create value and grow its financial performance on a sustainable basis. In the knowledge era, our belief is that the best way to attain breakthrough performance is by building a conductive organization where sustainable financial capital growth is based on the organization's ability to grow its customer capital. And customer capital generation requires that the organization's structural and human capital are fully aligned to value creation at the customer interface.

We've found it useful to describe how one capital dimension interacts with another and how they interact holistically through what we call the Knowledge Capital Model. This model has been key to our work at both Clarica and Armstrong—and has been greatly influenced by the work of Karl-Erik Sueiby and Leif Edvinsson.

Throughout the rest of the book, we describe many of the principles, tools, and techniques that we've found useful in growing customer, human, and structural capital. Although, for ease of explanation, each dimension is discussed separately, from our experience they should be understood holistically. It's only through their interaction that value is created.

Intangible Assets

In today's business context, an organization's value proposition (i.e., what creates value in the organization) has radically changed.

Intangible assets are not often recognized as a component of an organization's collective assets (see Figure 3.1). However, these intangible assets (i.e., knowledge capital) play a key role in capability generation. They are the result of learning that take place within the organization and between the organization and its customers.

We describe intangible assets in terms of:

Human capital: the attributes, competencies, and mindsets of the individuals who make up an organization. The individual capabilities of an organization serve to build organizational capabilities and create value for customers.

Structural capital: the strategies, structures, processes, culture, and leadership that translate into specific core competencies of the organization (e.g., the ability to develop solutions, manage risk, engineer processes, understand markets). Organizational capabilities leverage individual capabilities in creating value for customers.

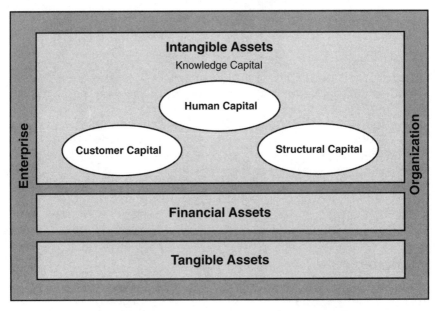

Figure 3.1 Types of Assets in an Organization

Customer capital: the sum of all customer relationships, defined as the depth (penetration or share of wallet), breadth (coverage or share of market), sustainability (durability), and profitability of the organization's relationships with all of its customers. While customer capital includes all external relationships, we focus on customers and suppliers—not all stakeholders. Our goal is to focus on people directly involved in value creation for the customer and the organization.

Our challenge is that the overall blueprint of today's organization has, for the most part, been inherited from the industrial era, leaving organizations ill equipped to manage their intangible assets.

The Knowledge Capital Model

The Knowledge Capital Model (see Figure 3.2) provides a new perspective for managing the intangible assets in an organization—for systematically developing, maintaining, leveraging, and renewing them. An organization creates value when individual employees interact with customers. The quality of these relationships will determine the effect on the organization's customer capital. The structural capital interacts directly with customer capital but also serves mainly as the platform from which human capital can increase the value created for customers. In other words, structural

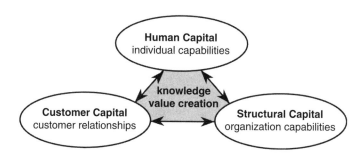

Figure 3.2 Knowledge Capital Model

capital provides employees with the organizational support they need to offer added value to customers.

We've made two key assumptions when creating this model:

1. *An organization's intangible assets are made of capabilities and relationships that are built through the exchange of knowledge.*

   Value creation occurs as knowledge flows among the three types of knowledge capital. Knowledge exchange serves as the basis for accelerating learning and systematically developing individual and organizational capabilities. It's essential that we promote and facilitate the free flow of knowledge across the organization. Achieving higher levels of conductivity relies on an organization's ability to establish trust through relationships. Trust determines the bandwidth of knowledge exchange and the extent of the value creation potential.

2. *An organization's intangible assets form a system that must be managed through an integrated approach.*

   It's pointless to try and manage customer relationships in isolation from the development of individual and organizational capabilities. All three forms of capital (human, structural, and customer) should be developed and maintained in an integrated approach.

The Enterprise Capital Model

At Armstrong, we modified The Knowledge Capital Model and developed a new model that we call The Enterprise Capital Model (see Figure 3.3). Our belief is that value can't be created for an organization or its customers if human, structural, and customer capital operate in isolation. Without interaction, there is only *value in waiting*. Instead, we need to increase the interaction and alignment among these three forms of intangible assets in order to create value.

Human capital, for example, is often viewed as a stand-alone entity. But actually, it's incapable of creating value without the support of the organization's structural capital or interaction with

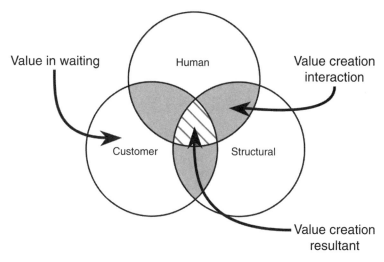

Figure 3.3 Armstrong's Enterprise Capital Model

customers. An organization can recruit the brightest and best in its sector, but if an internal process, structural configuration, or poor leadership blocks them, the organization's employees will provide little value to anyone, least of all to their customers.

Similarly, any attempt to build structural capital without considering human capital is bound to fail. We need only look at the fallout of ill-conceived or overly zealous downsizing or reengineering programs to be reminded of the need for human capital to interact with structural capital.

Value Creation and Depletion

Our experience has also led us to conclude that value is either created or depleted with every single interaction among the knowledge capital elements. Each one of the millions of interactions that take place every day within a global organization and with its customers and partners in value creation networks creates or depletes value. For example, customer capital is created when there is a high-quality knowledge exchange between individual employees and customers—between human capital and customer capital. This is conductivity at the customer interface.

Value creation is further assured when the structural capital of the corporation is configured to support employees in the delivery of added value to the customer. This action may be as simple as ensuring that customer-facing processes are designed so that each employee can make real-time decisions with customers without securing approval from the management hierarchy.

Conversely, customer capital is depleted whenever a customer has a poor contact with an organization's employee or when the structural capital of the organization is poorly configured to meet customer needs. For example, if a customer telephones a call center and the employee has incomplete information about that customer or the customer is passed between departments and has to continually repeat the nature of the enquiry, customer capital will erode, thereby putting financial capital at risk.

Clarica Example

Recognizing the interrelationships among these three dimensions can provide corporate leaders with a powerful early warning signal of potential problems. For example, in the late 1990s, Clarica acquired the Canadian operations of MetLife. Due to the process reengineering required to merge the companies, the quality of customer service declined for a while (the reshaping of structural capital was impacting the exchange of knowledge at the customer interface).

Clarica's chief executive officer, Bob Astley, commented that this, albeit short-term, reduction in service quality was a matter of real concern. Eventually the company would pay for it in financial terms. The CEO's concern led to a series of interventions geared to accelerate the integration of operations from MetLife into Clarica with an increased focus on providing quality customer service. This example of a leader recognizing the dependencies between customer and financial capital—how they are intertwined—reflects an understanding of the increased attention to intangible assets in the knowledge era.

Stocks and Flows

Stocks and flows power the dynamic of the Knowledge Capital Model. Stocks represent the accumulated individual capabilities (human capital), organizational capabilities (structural capital), and customer relationships (customer capital). Stocks can be described as the amount or volume of capital that has been created through generating capabilities. They are to a large degree measurable and visible. A long-term relationship with a customer and a repository of customer information are examples of stocks.

Flows are what happen between the stocks and what impel the creation or depletion of stocks. Flows are the exchange of knowledge between individuals in the organization and between the organization and its customers or partners in order to build new capabilities and deepen relationships. The conductive organization uses its existing capabilities and generates new capabilities to enable unimpeded knowledge flow, which in turn creates new stocks, increasing the organization's intangible assets.

How stocks flow depends on the type of knowledge that is being conducted. *Explicit knowledge* is knowledge that has been articulated or codified in words or numbers, such as tools, procedures, and templates. Explicit knowledge sharing is enhanced by technology to ensure that knowledge is captured and accessible throughout the organization.

Tacit knowledge is the intuitions, perspectives, beliefs, values, and know-how that result from the experience of individual employees and of the organization as a whole. Unlike explicit knowledge, tacit knowledge encompasses things people know but that are not documented anywhere. It's frequently communicated through conversations with the use of metaphors. Know-how, understanding, mental models, insights, and principles inherent to a discipline are all tacit knowledge. Tacit knowledge is shared personally through work teams or structures such as communities of practice, where people with shared interests come together to exchange knowledge and create solutions.

A knowledge architecture supports the dynamic interchange of stocks by a variety of methods. A knowledge strategy defines how the conductive organization encourages knowledge creation and exchange. It guides how new and existing knowledge is used to enhance capabilities. It also provides the vision and direction for investing in knowledge capital. The knowledge architecture provides the blueprint for achieving the knowledge strategy's goals—it outlines the approaches for placing the collective knowledge of the organization at the disposal of everyone.

Knowledge access and knowledge exchange are two components of the architecture that support the flow of tacit and explicit knowledge (see Figure 3.4). As we noted above, tacit knowledge is best exchanged between people, while explicit knowledge should be accessed with the support of technology. We'll talk more about these components in our discussion of learning and collaborating in chapter 9.

Flows have similar attributes to tacit knowledge. They are both people-based and can prove challenging to capture and articulate. Stocks are much more like explicit knowledge in that they are visible and accessible. A challenge for corporate leaders is to create the

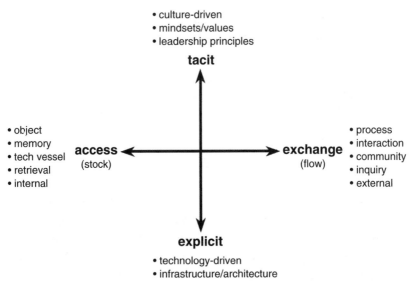

Figure 3.4 Knowledge Stocks and Flows

capabilities for the organization to enable the exchange of tacit knowledge and access to explicit knowledge—no small leadership task, given the historical context of most organizations and their leadership environments.

Influences on Value Creation and Depletion

Influences on value creation or depletion change at each interface between the elements of the Knowledge Capital Model—at points between human and customer capital, structural and customer capital, and structural and human capital (see Tables 3.1, 3.2, and 3.3). These influences can be discussed in terms of attractors and detractors—the pluses and minuses of particular influences. We use the term *attractors* to describe organizational characteristics that we believe create capital and *detractors* to describe characteristics that deplete capital.

Table 3.1 Creating or Depleting Capital at the Human Capital-Customer Capital Interface

Attractors	Detractors
Personal responsibility of employees for customer relationships	Internal preoccupation
Customer-focus and quality service orientation	Insulated from customer contact
Active learning with customers	Inability to relate to customers
Continuity in role	High level of attrition change in customer-facing staff
Responsiveness	Lack of responsiveness
Commitment to shared purpose	Lack of alignment in actions
Self-initiation—ownership of one's rote in the enterprise	Feeling of entitlement
Sense-and-respond perspective	Make-and-sell perspective
Alignment of competencies to customer requirements	Competency gaps
Well-stated and understood strategies	Lack of strategic clarity
Solutions correspond with customer needs	Inappropriate solutions

Table 3.2 Creating or Depleting Capital at the Structural Capital-Customer Capital Interface

Attractors	Detractors
Well-tuned business processes geared to the customer	Inefficient or ineffective processes not geared to the customer
Win-win service orientation to customer	Lack of connection and feedback loops with customers
Simplified, streamlined structure aligned to customer relationships	Internally generated turbulence
Harvesting as opposed to distributing knowledge	Insufficient or inaccurate technical support
Learning with the customer as an inherent part of service	Learning focused only on internal needs
Products as building blocks for innovative solutions for the customer	Predominance of product orientation versus solution orientation

Table 3.3 Creating or Depleting Capital at the Structural Capital-Human Capital Interface

Attractors	Detractors
Shared sense of purpose organization	Segmented (stove-pipe)
Entrepreneurial culture fostering individual initiative	Bureaucratic barriers
Cohesiveness through strategic bonding	High proportion of low customer value activity
Alignment of strategic capability elements	Lack of customer visibility
Dynamic leadership and managerial courage	Strategic confusion
Speed of change and agility	Static and inflexible position Centralized leadership and decision-making
Emphasis on learning and innovation	Limited interest in learning, either internally or with the customer
Articulated values	Unarticulated values

Creating capital at the customer interface requires committed, self-initiated, customer-focused employees willing to learn and co-develop solutions with customers and across functional units internally. As a consequence, value is created for the employees and the customers, and ultimately for the organization. And once again, we see generalized reciprocity—the give-and-take flow of knowledge in a trusting relationship—functioning as part of the conductivity within the organization and between the organization and its customers and partners.

We find that self-initiation is essential to the development of highly committed employees focused on creating value for the customer. Self-initiated employees have a strong sense of ownership over their performance, their career, and their learning. This strong sense of ownership is a precondition to the employees having a strong sense of ownership for the value they create for the customer. Self-initiation is enabled by a culture in which the individual employee takes responsibility for growing his or her own capabilities through learning, collaborating, and knowledge exchange.

Creating capital at the structural-customer capital interface requires customer-calibrated internal processes and structures. Customer calibration calls for a customer service orientation and leveraging of technology to capture and exchange customer information as well as the knowledge gained from learning with the customer.

Capital at the structural-human capital interface is generated by ensuring that the organization's culture is supportive of its aspirations—the individual employees think strategically with a full understanding of the organization's imperatives and the customers' needs. At this intersection, leadership has a significant role in cementing this customer-facing strategic mindset.

Viewing these three tables together, we see that there is a critical cultural underpinning to the creation of capital at all three interfaces. It's safe to say that the organization's culture serves as the key determinant of value creation as well as a significant variable for producing a highly conductive organization. Generating knowledge capital in an organization depends on the alignment of the organization's culture to the values of the employees and the expectations of customers. This can best be achieved though the development of a values-based approach to leadership guiding everyone's behaviour within the organization and with all external stakeholders.

Strategic Risk

We've found that getting a sense of the attractors and detractors within the capital interfaces is a useful way to gain a strong sense of the strategic risk that the corporation faces. For example, seeing problems such as erosion of the customer base or an inability to cope with marketplace change makes it possible to design effective interventions—to recalibrate the organization.

An inability to relate to customers (a human-customer capital detractor), combined with inefficient or ineffective processes not geared to the customer (a structural-customer capital detractor) and a high proportion of low customer value activity (a structural-human capital detractor) certainly signals a high probability of strategic failure.

Conversely, a personal responsibility of employees for customer relationships (a human-customer capital attractor), combined with a simplified, streamlined structure aligned to customer relationships (a customer-structural capital attractor) and speed of change and agility (a structural-human capital attractor) suggests a high likelihood of strategic success.

The conductive organization strives to mitigate strategic risk by building the capabilities required to operate the corporation from the attractors' column and replace any characteristics that function as detractors. Once again, note the influence of culture that appears in each of the attractor columns. Managing strategic risk is underpinned by on-going efforts to enhance cultural cohesion. In addition, the effective management of risk requires continuous organizational, customer, and individual learning. Learning—the ability to turn information into knowledge for effective action—is something we continually return to throughout this book and in our lives.

Measurement

Over recent years, tracking strategic risk has led to an explosion in strategic performance measurement. It's thought that by placing metrics around customer processes and employee performance, we can get a handle on how likely we are to successfully implement corporate strategies. This is the central premise of Kaplan and Norton's hugely popular balanced scorecard strategic management framework and methodology. The scorecard sets out to describe a cause and affect relationship between strategic objectives and measures from the employee perspective through internal, customer, and financial perspectives. (1)

So where does performance measurement fit within the Knowledge Capital Model? We stated in Chapter 2 that we are cautious about relying too heavily on measures of customer satisfaction and loyalty. Equally, our experience makes us circumspect about measurement generally, especially when it comes to keeping track of the relationship between stocks and flows.

As an analogy of the measurement conundrum, visualize someone drawing a bucket of water from a river. The bucketful of water is the stock but it doesn't tell us anything about the flow of the river. We can measure this stock by its amount (weight and volume) and by its quality (purity or pollution). But we have no idea whether the flow will enable us to create new stocks into the future. Will the river's flow support the continued withdrawal of water? There's a danger in viewing stock metrics in isolation from flow— of taking the stock out of the context of the flow.

However, this isn't to say there is no value in measuring stocks. Managers are duty bound to take an interest in the outcome of actions, and stock measures do provide some indications of how successful knowledge flows are at creating value. There are many stock measures that we can use. For example:

Human Capital
- Actual competence level versus the ideal level to attain
- Supply/demand ratios in succession planning

- Completed development plans
- Capability for team work
- Ability to develop and maintain relationships both internally and with customers or partners
- Percentage of new ideas that are actually implemented.

Structural Capital
- Cost per transaction
- Percentage of cost reduction
- Revenue per employee
- Cycle time and cost improvement of main business processes
- Rate of process improvement index
- Number of new products each year.

Customer Capital
- Satisfaction indices
- Reduction of complaint resolution time
- Percentage of penetration and coverage
- Longevity of relationships
- Perception of comparative value-added
- Price sensitivity
- Customer profitability
- Financial well being of long-term customers.

Although these measures are useful, they're lagging performance measures in that they essentially tell us what has already happened and don't in themselves necessarily tell us what *will* happen in the future. For example, a measure of customer profitability tells us what was achieved in the previous accounting periods and not what will happen in the next.

Armstrong Example

Using the Enterprise Capital Model, we've experimented with ways to identify useful leading performance indicators by calculating the value-creating opportunity afforded by the interactions among knowledge capital elements. This is certainly work in progress. What we have been experimenting with is calculating the rate at which value is being created or how value-in-waiting is being converted into actual value.

Specifically, we've been experimenting at Armstrong with measuring the level of knowledge transfer risk associated with various forms of product or service development. The driving concern is the amount of resources and effort required to reduce the knowledge transfer risk to make the product successful in the marketplace. We've tried to quantify the risk associated with providing customers with the knowledge they need before they'll decide to purchase a new product. This metric is generated by looking at the knowledge flow effectiveness from the development team, through the organization, to the distribution system, and finally to the customer. The greater the knowledge loss in the process of transmission or the more resistance likely to be experienced to a new product or service introduction, the higher the knowledge transfer risk.

Knowledge transfer risk can be managed in part through developing more conductive capabilities in the organization, including improving knowledge access and exchange (e.g., web-based technical information, phone access to application specialists dedicated to the new product development, access to a referral network). As well, we need to continuously fine-tune our calibration with the customer. Customers need to play a key role in designing solutions.

We can illustrate this approach with a knowledge transfer risk assessment that we developed for a number of different types of product development activities from pure research and design (R&D) to simple product fixes. Figure 3.5 charts our knowledge transfer risk assessment for a particular product development cycle.

The project is rated for its return or reward and technical risk factors on the vertical axis and the knowledge transfer risk to enable the customer to act and purchase the new product on the horizontal axis. The metric draws on the current wisdom in the organization and acts as a proxy for conductivity as it relates to new product

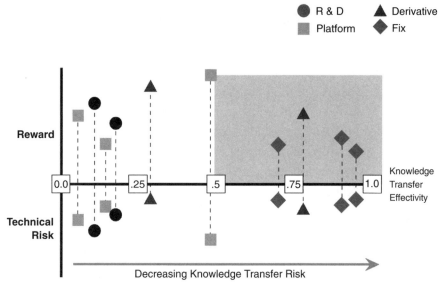

Figure 3.5   Knowledge Transfer Risk

development. We've found the measurement approach useful in managing factors that, if not attended to, could lead to product introduction failures.

Conclusion

We've found the Knowledge Capital Model to be a simple model that helps people understand what we mean by the intangible stocks and flows of knowledge—the basis of conductivity in an organization. It can provide a rallying point, a map of cause and effect that customers and employees can understand. It helps us make sense of this new form of value that for some still remains a mystery.

The Knowledge Capital Model is a straightforward framework on which other frameworks can hang (see Figure 3.6).

As we work through our ideas on how to build a highly conductive organization, this model acts as a foundation for the majority of our approaches. It's a central theme that sets the stage for looking

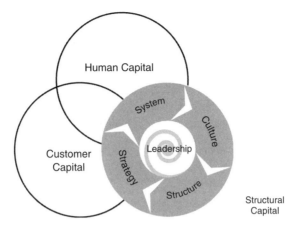

Figure 3.6 Merged Capital Models

at our organizations' assets with a new perspective. We suggest that, in order to achieve breakthrough performance, an organization must increase the effectiveness of the five key components of its structural capital: strategy, culture, structure, systems, and leadership.

Emerging Principles

- It's only through the interaction of human, structural, and customer capital that value is created.

- An organization's intangible assets are made of capabilities and relationships that are built through the exchange of knowledge.

- A challenge for corporate leaders is to create the capabilities for the organization to enable the exchange of tacit knowledge and the access to explicit knowledge.

- The adoption of values-based leadership throughout an organization will lead to greater alignment and enhance the creation of value through knowledge exchange.

- Intangible assets now represent the most important source of value.

- An organization's intangible assets form a system that must be managed through an integrated, values-based approach.

- Value is either created or depleted with every single interaction among the knowledge capital elements.

Reference

1. Kaplan, R.S. and D.P. Norton (2001). *The Strategy-Focused Organization: How Balanced Scorecard Companies Thrive in the New Business Environment.* Boston: Harvard Business School Press.

4

Customer Calibration

Introduction

Calibration is generally understood as an act of adjustment to a standard. Customer calibration is the process by which an organization continually adjusts its strategies and capabilities to an ever-rising standard demanded by the customer (e.g., service level, product integration, relationship requirements). For the conductive organization customer calibration is not an episodic reconfiguration—a regular six-month "tune up." Instead, it's a constant process that informs all of the organization's thinking, actions, and relationships, enabled by the quality and speed of its knowledge flow.

Customer calibration requires that the highly conductive organization possess an intimate, tacit understanding of the customer. In our experience, such an intimate customer relationship is difficult to create without deep levels of trust between the organization and its customers. As we explain in this chapter and the next, it's only in a climate of trust that mutually beneficial customer learning can take place, that knowledge can flow, and, ultimately, that an organization can be considered highly conductive.

Relationship Levels

Some corporate leaders and their employees may find it difficult to view their customer relationships in terms of partnering. We suggest that there are four different levels of relationships with customers: partnering, business solutions, product solutions, and transactions (see Figure 4.1).

As a rule, closer partnering between a customer and a supplier will create greater value for both. However, the optimal level of a relationship will depend on the capabilities and the predispositions of both the customer and supplier organizations. Whether an organization is more or less predisposed to partnering will depend in large part on its internal culture. An organization whose culture emphasizes internal collaboration, synergy, and interdependence will likely place greater value on relationships that are at the higher end of the partnering spectrum. Arriving at the right level of relationship is essentially a matching process.

The customer must be able to realize the value offered by a partnering supplier. As well, the supplier must have the capability to

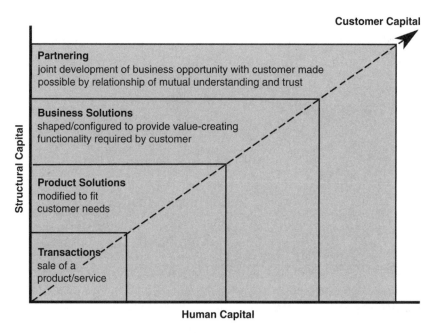

Figure 4.1 Levels of Customer Relationships

build and maintain a relationship at a given level on the partnering spectrum. In many ways, this is a dance led by the customer. Some customers are more sensitive to the value creation brought by closer relationships with their suppliers and are more predisposed to partnering with them. If the supplier that invests in building a closer relationship with a customer isn't predisposed to higher levels of collaboration, the customer won't be able to recognize and exploit the potential value of such a relationship. The supplier will then incur additional costs that won't represent value to the customer.

Competitive Pressures and Customer Levels

Although exponentially rising competition is pressuring profit margins at all relationship levels, these pressures are most pronounced at the transactional level, where products and services are most easily replicated and pricing most easily improved upon. When a supplier can achieve a higher level of relationship with a customer, the customer can more easily differentiate the offerings between competitors and will be more likely to stay with this supplier rather than moving to one of its competitors. Smart leaders, whether of high-tech or low-tech, business-to-business, or business-to-consumer organizations, will figure out how to compete at or near the partnering level.

Clarica, for example, competed in a financial services sector that is typically viewed closer to the transactional than the partnering level. However, Clarica set out to differentiate itself in a crowded marketplace with a partnering-based strategy. Partnership (internal and external) became a core value, and significant resources were dedicated to generating capabilities and engendering partnering mindsets, both within the company and with its customers and partners. This was confirmed with the brand promise *clarity through dialogue*. In all interactions with customers and other shareholders, Clarica consistently represented itself as wanting to build relationships based on trust and high levels of collaboration.

Innovation

Building customer relationships based on partnering goes hand-in-hand with *innovation*, which we describe as sharing information and creating knowledge to constantly find new ways to deliver relevant, high-quality solutions to our customers. Characteristic of a highly conductive organization, innovation relies on the ability to increase capabilities in real time to ensure that solutions (external) and processes (internal) are aligned to meet the customer's needs.

An innovative organization differs from both a traditional and a leading organization (see Figure 4.2). Note how an innovative organization creates and shapes the market, as opposed to a traditional organization that serves the market and a leading organization that leads the market in new directions. In terms of customer impact, a traditional organization focuses on customer retention, a leading organization on customer satisfaction, and an innovative organization on customer success. The higher the customer relationship level the organization attains, the more it requires the capability to innovate.

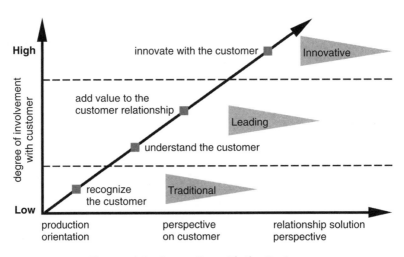

Figure 4.2 Innovating with the Customer

We can look in more detail at the differences between these three types of organizations and their characteristics in the following Table 4.1.

Table 4.1 Characteristics of Traditional, Leading, and Innovative Organizations

Element	Traditional	Leading	Innovative
Market	Serves the market	Leads the market	Creates/shapes the market
Stakeholders	Internally oriented	Recognition of multiple stakeholders	Partnership with stakeholders
Approach to customer	Internally driven	Segmentation of market offerings	Co-developed solutions
Regulatory	Comply	Pushes the boundaries	Contributes to shape rules
Processes	Based on business lines	Fee for integrated service	Cross-functional integration
Technology	Centralized gatekeeper	Integration with internal business users	Integration with customer systems
Offerings	Transactions, products	Integrated solutions	Innovative solutions based on customer perceived value
Focus	Market share	Customer relationships	Strategic partnerships with customers
Customer Impact	Customer retention	Customer satisfaction	Customer success

Listening to the Customer

Partnering and innovation require capabilities to talk with the customers in new ways, to listen to customers, and to act on what we hear. In the conductive organization, the objective is to build the capabilities to, ". . . amplify weak signals, interpret their consequences and reconfigure resources faster than competitors. . . ." (1)

In the article just cited, Prahalad and Ramaswamy make the observation that, largely due to the Internet, the opportunities for consumers to enter into active and explicit conversations with suppliers have increased enormously. "What's more the dialogue is no longer being controlled by corporations. Individual consumers can address and learn about businesses either on their own or through the collective knowledge of other customers. Customers can now initiate the dialogue." (2)

The authors further state that, in the new marketplace, organizations must also recognize that their dialogue with the customer is a dialogue of equals. They suggest that engaging in a dialogue with customers who know what they want requires richer and subtler forms of exchange than most organizations are used to.

Our experience supports these observations, and our concepts of generative capabilities, customer calibration, and conductivity essentially embody the amplification, interpretation, and reconfiguration processes required to engage the customer at a level of conversation that is truly meaningful.

Rich customer conversations work at many levels and serve as the valve for unimpeded knowledge flow and continuous learning at the customer interface. Customer conversations are most effective when they are solution or aspiration driven as opposed to product focused. The goal is to discover the problems customers are trying to solve or the goals they are working toward.

On one level customer relationship management systems are useful tools that provide immediate access to customer information that can be used to find out more about the customers' aspirations and needs. When these tools and other technological systems are linked through a knowledge strategy with employees who have the capabilities to deepen customer relationships, then rich conversations ensue. The possibility of providing a new solution for the customer is increased. The unarticulated business need has then been identified, and the organization has the opportunity to establish first-mover advantage.

Mindsets at Mayekawa Manufacturing Co., Ltd.

On another level, solution-based customer conversations require a more fundamental mindset shift within the host organization. Consider the Japanese industrial refrigeration specialist Mayekawa Manufacturing Co., Ltd.

A central tenet of Mayekawa Manufacturing's relationship with its customers is what its president Mr. Masao Maekawa describes as "gapless co-experiencing with the customer." (3) He believes that this co-experiencing requires that the organization "indwell in the world of the customers, to achieve a oneness of subject and object; this helps to understand the needs of the customer."

According to Mr. Masao Maekawa, gapless co-experiencing requires that the relationship with the customer not be dominated by the company's own ideas; rather, representatives adopt what Maekawa describes as "an unfiltered mindset" in which the possible customer solutions that enter the representatives' minds are not limited by Mayekawa Manufacturing's own product designs. The organization is not a conventional sales or product supplier—it exhibits many dimensions of a highly conductive organization.

What this means in practical terms is that Mayekawa Manufacturing's representatives don't enter into a conversation with a customer, or potential customer, blinkered by a focus on selling a product (in this case an industrial freezer), but try to understand the problem the customer is dealing with. To do this effectively, the representative has to understand what it means to see through the eyes of the customer or "indwell in the world of the customers." In doing so, they are able to enter the marketplace and compete from within the elusive, yet lucrative, unarticulated and unserved customer dimension we discussed in Chapter 2.

Mayekawa Manufacturing worked with one customer whose articulated requirement was for an industrial refrigeration solution for use in a chicken processing facility—a seemingly simple need for an industrial refrigeration manufacturer to fulfill. However, in working to understand the dynamics of the customer's operation (the indwelling), Mayekawa Manufacturing discovered that the customer had a significant problem with chicken de-boning.

In the end, Mayekawa Manufacturing developed a technological solution for chicken de-boning that linked to refrigeration. Not only did this solution meet an unarticulated/unserved need of that customer, it also provided Mayekawa Manufacturing with a capability of enormous value to the chicken processing industry, one that could not be easily replicated by its competitors. In short, Mayekawa Manufacturing had created a new capability for itself and its customer by competing from the partnering level. Moreover, it was shaping a new market.

Armstrong Example—The Customer Dialer

Armstrong created a tool that helps develop new ways of engaging our customers in meaningful conversations called the Customer Dialer. It's enabled the organization to increase our capability to calibrate to our customers. The idea came from a strategy session where we explored ways to wrap our company around our customers—to be more engaged with customers and increase knowledge stocks and flows. Using the Customer Dialer, managers were able to break through our traditional silos and work in a cross-functional way to strengthen the product and service offerings, aligning them more closely to customer requirements.

The Customer Dialer (see Figure 4.3) is a collaborative tool for identifying customer requirements and matching Armstrong's capabilities to these needs, for co-creating business solutions, and for evolving new capabilities. The Customer Dialer (3) has been customized for each of the customer clusters and can be further customized to meet unique needs of individual customers.

The Customer Dialer has four concentric circles outlining customer needs, touchpoints, current capabilities, and upcoming or evolving capabilities. But an important function of the Customer Dialer is that it provides customers a menu of options through

Figure 4.3 Armstrong's Customer Dialer

which they can relate to Armstrong, giving customers a sense of ownership of the choices they're making and the solutions they're creating.

Customer Needs

At the center of the Customer Dialer sits the customer, in this example a design-build contractor. This configuration in itself depicts Armstrong's long-held belief that the customer is at the heart of all we do.

Through a process of discussion and investigation, the requirements of the customer are identified. To extend the conversation, we provide each customer with a workbook tailored to that customer group. Customers are asked to identify their greatest needs, the challenges they face, and their biggest concerns. They're also asked to describe what success would look like for each identified requirement. In an effort to unearth those needs, Armstrong employees review the information in face-to-face sessions with customers.

Of course, there are many ways to probe customer requirements. Some of the most effective are remarkably low-tech. At Armstrong, we run evening sessions with customers to discuss their needs, aspirations, and fears with our senior managers. This type of conversation will only work when there is a high level of mutual trust between the customer and the organization. These relaxed, informal conversations provide a wealth of valuable information. Specifically, we gain a greater understanding of intangibles such as how the customer views risk in a building project or frustration in trying to preserve the environment while at the same time meeting cost expectations. We uncover the as-yet unarticulated and unmet needs of our customers and have successfully co-developed solutions that gave us first-mover advantage.

Customer Touchpoints

With customer needs identified, we move to the next circle of the Customer Dialer—the ring of tiles that represent the all-important *customer touchpoints*. Touchpoints are the contact points between Armstrong and our customers and their business. They're the means by which Armstrong employees are able to communicate and collaborate with our customers—through a call center, site maintenance, regional training, catalogues, webinars, and face-to-face interactions.

The touchpoints aren't just a static list of customer avenues. They're the connectors with which Armstrong can establish conductivity at the customer interface—the places where knowledge flows between our customers and our business.

Current Capabilities

Moving out from touchpoints, we find Armstrong's current capabilities. For the purpose of the Customer Dialer, capabilities are defined as the skills, tools, and value-creation opportunities that the organization offers to its customers and partners, such as application support, after-sales support, Armstrong University, and our extranet.

Most of these capabilities are what you might consider as adding intangible value—things not expected by our customers. They are tools that support learning, collaboration, and strategy making that in turn increase our capabilities to build partnering relationships and spark innovation. We believe by investing in these types of tools we increase our customer capital and distinguish ourselves in the marketplace.

- **Armstrong University** is a forum, offered several times a year, in which the organization gathers different groups together from our customer community. During these sessions we explore customers' requirements and co-create solutions that address these needs. The format includes workshops and technical learning programs.
- **Armstrong Catalogue Expert**, or ACE, is proprietary software that gives customers direct access to full technical specifications. ACE was a first in the industry, created specifically to meet customer needs. Specification selection is based on personalized criteria, embedded application knowledge, and analyses of system design, energy efficiency, submittals, drawings, quotations, and on-line ordering.
- **Armlink** is a collaborative environment that allows the co-creation and sharing of crucial information surrounding the project and solution requirements in an online, interactive format.

The identified capabilities and touchpoint rings of the Dialer aren't static. They're in a constant state of change based on the changing needs of the customer.

Evolving Capabilities

The outer circle of the Customer Dialer represents upcoming or evolving capabilities. It serves to remind us that, to remain an industry leader, we must create new capabilities in real time and on an ongoing basis.

The Customer Dialer and Internal Dialoguing

We've found the Customer Dialer to be a useful tool for facilitating customer-focused conversations between our employees. We use it to enhance conductivity throughout our organization.

Employees from all functions and disciplines can see, discuss, and bring their own perspective to the customers' needs, capabilities, and touchpoints. The Customer Dialer is useful in showing how the work of all employees relates to the customer and in galvanizing their thinking about generating the capabilities we need to constantly improve customer service.

Every Armstrong employee participates in a learning session on the Customer Dialer. We've also started to use the Customer Dialer with our own suppliers, working to make explicit the capabilities of, and find complementarities within, our value-creation networks.

Value-Creation Networks and ValueNet Works™

Given the complex requirements of some solution development, a single organization may not be able to fully meet the customer's requirements. It needs to partner with other organizations, each bringing to the relationship a particular set of unique capabilities—capabilities that represent a special expertise.

One approach is to develop a multiple-participant network that creates value for the customer based on each organization's contribution of a specific capability domain in which it has a clear advantage. These networks can be successful because each organization participating in the network:

- Understands the value of the network strategy
- Knows their customers' needs
- Has the capabilities to partner
- Can leverage technology to realize their strategy.

The value-creation network provides a collective way of knowing—the result of sharing knowledge across the network. It also forms a new way of creating value, leveraging intangible as well as tangible value.

ValueNet Works™, a tool developed with Verna Allee, who is a thought leader on effectively using knowledge in the new economy, allows organizations, their customers, and their partners to identify complementary or value-adding capabilities by mapping both tangible and intangible exchanges among members of a value-creation network. (4)

The ValueNet Works™ system defines tangibles as products or services that are paid for and therefore expected within the relationship. Intangibles are the extras, or the value-adding services, typically concerning knowledge exchange among members of the network, that are not paid for or possibly not even well articulated. To illustrate the ValueNet Works™ analytic process, review a value network map for one of Armstrong's customer clusters (see Figure 4.4). The participants are all involved in a conventional building project that includes creating specifications, bidding on the project, and then building the product.

The key members of the value-creation network are the designated nodes—the manufacturer (in this case Armstrong), a consulting engineer, and a building owner. A solid black line represents the tangible exchanges (e.g., an order from contractor to manufacturer and a product from manufacturer to contractor). The intangible exchange is represented by the dotted line (e.g., the technology

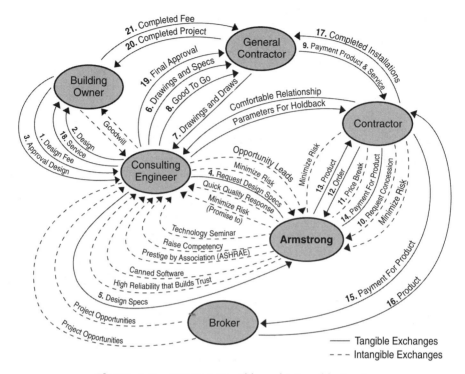

Figure 4.4   Mapping Tangible and Intangible Assets

seminars and design assistance from manufacturer to consulting engineer).

The point of this mapping exercise is to help the organization view the added-value proposition it makes to customers. It shows the benefits that Armstrong derives from its partners and identifies the additional added-value exchanges that can be initiated. It also gives a bird's eye view of the many relationships created among all nodes of the value-creation network.

Value is created from both types of exchanges—tangible and intangible. However, without taking the time to identify the exchanges, the value that results from the intangible exchanges in particular may never be fully realized. For example, the high degree of reliability that results from the exchange between the consulting engineer and the manufacturer (see solid black line 5) during the development of design specifications increases the level of trust. More intangibles that create value flow from this interaction, including: goodwill, a high-quality relationship, minimalized risk, and improved speed and quality of response.

Because Armstrong is working with its customers to fashion new solutions, it is cognizant of the tangible and intangible requirements of each node and can factor these requirements into the solution being created. For example, Armstrong thinks not only of the engineer creating the building design, but also the contractor who will have to install it, the building owner who will have to pay for it, the building operator who will have to run equipment, and the corporate or private residents of the building who will be the end-users. All those needs, along with Armstrong's technical requirements, are among the considerations for creating a viable solution in partnership with all members of the value-creation network, including the customers.

Intangibles as a Competitive Differentiator

The benefit of mapping intangibles is that they represent an organization's competitive differentiators. Competitors may be able to replicate tangible products or service dimensions, but they'll find it extremely difficult to replicate the intangibles, the value-adding dimensions that help deepen the relationship with customers. Customers will readily recognize that they cannot easily get these extras from another company, so a competitive advantage is created for the conductive organization. These intangibles are a significant contributor to raising the organization's relationships to the partnering level discussed earlier and into the domain of generalized reciprocity— once again, key dimensions of a highly conductive organization.

Leveraging the Distribution Network

In discussing the customer value-creation network, one factor we should spend time considering is the distribution network. Distributors have a massive impact at the customer interface, so we must consider them a key factor in enhancing the transmission rate and quality of knowledge flow. An organization may understand its markets and may be developing new products based on good customer understanding, but the products may hit the distribution channel and fail because of a lack of trust and partnership between distributors and customers or distributors and the organization.

For many organizations, the distribution channel is the ultimate bottleneck in the flow of knowledge between the organization and the customer. However, distribution should be a critical part of the organization's ability to create value. In fact, the relationship between the host organization and its distribution agents constitutes a significant part of their respective structural capital. The economic value of both organization and distributor depends to a large extent on how effective they are at partnering with each other and at presenting a unified face to the customer.

Interdependence

Achieving an effective win-win partnership requires an interdependent relationship between the organization and its distributors. Too often the organization-distributor relationship becomes counterdependent, and those who should be partners question everything the other does.

From a business perspective, this means that one party actively denies the value that the other party brings to the relationship. One party is always second-guessing the other's motive because it believes it's being taken advantage of—a dynamic state that works both ways. For example, in the petroleum industry, independent dealers may sell gasoline and get a percentage of the margin. But when oil companies are constantly squeezing the margins, the relationship becomes counterdependent.

With interdependence, however, both parties realize that their relationship will produce the most value through close collaboration and trust.

Clarica Example—Independent Agents

Clarica had a distribution network of about 3,000 self-employed agents who, on a daily basis, interacted with the customer at a personal, face-to-face level. For all intents and purposes, these agents *were* Clarica in the eyes of the customer. Therefore, it was the agents who had to deliver Clarica's brand promise of *clarity through dialogue*. Recognizing the absolute importance of its agents, Clarica invested substantial time and energy in ensuring that the agents felt they were a critical part of the Clarica experience.

Although independent business owners, the agents participated in the same values-based surveys and analyses as Clarica employees to ensure that the core values expressed by agents were congruent with those of the organization and its employees. Clarica also helped support a community of practice for agents so that they could benefit from knowledge exchange. And to enhance conductivity, Clarica established a dedicated agent's web portal.

Clarica understood that, by creating the right culture and infrastructure, they made it possible for their agents to show commitment to and a sense of ownership of the relationship with the customer. Aligning agents would go a long way to mitigating any risk of strategic failure—the central role of agents in the execution of Clarica's strategies was explicitly recognized. Building trust, therefore, became critical to the relationship.

Trust and the Distribution Network

As with customer-supplier relationships the distributor-organization relationship can only develop in a high-trust environment. The prerequisites to working interdependently and collaboratively are high-quality sharing, listening, and mutual trust. Such an environment is conducive to co-experiencing one another's dilemmas, difficulties, and issues. The organization hears the customer's perspective through the distributor. The distributor hears the organization's perspective directly from the organization. And the distributor can then translate that perspective to the customer so that the customer perceives value in the organization's offerings.

Conversations with Distributors

For the host organization-distributor relationship to work fully, the leaders of the host organization must listen closely to what their distributors tell them. After all, the distributors are generally closest to the customer and can pick up on changing customer aspirations and requirements.

We've found it makes sense that these conversations center on generating customer capital and deepening the organization's knowledge of the customer, without either party's being defensive about who owns the customer. When both the host organization and the distributor focus on the interests of the customer, they discover their true common interests and can identify a common perspective. In a sense, when counterdependence is evident, it is because such an exchange is seen as a zero-sum game where the competing interest of the two partners becomes the focus. In this case, the parties need to consider how they can collaborate to create more value together in a value network than any single competitor could create on its own.

Values Congruence

It's important to select distributors whose values and customer perspective are congruent with the host organization's values and perspective. A common perspective forms the foundation on which the relationship can be soundly established and grow over time. A misalignment of values, vision, and strategies between the host organization and distributor will typically undermine the organization's customer capital.

Successful partnerships are based on interdependent relationships in which all parties have the confidence and the sense of responsibility to take self-initiated action to solve problems and face challenges as they emerge. They're also relationships in which the respective partners' contributions are recognized and rewarded.

Being refocused on the customer can revitalize a distribution network that is old and established in its ways. The host organization should talk with the distributors about the customer and the value being created for the customer. All too often, the discussion between the host organization and distributor is about the arrangements between the two of them. Conversations that don't include the customer are barriers to conductivity. They impede the knowledge flow and reduce the opportunity to increase customer capital.

Internal and External Message Congruence

Finally, when we talk about customer calibration there must be a congruence of internal and external messages. You cannot have an internal message focused solely on selling to the customer at the highest possible price and an external message that puts the customer first and promises high-quality service. These messages are not consistent. And where incongruence exists, trust is not created and customer learning is not possible. This brings us to the importance of branding and the alignment of internal and external brand promises in the next chapter.

Conclusion

Calibrating the organization to its customers' needs is central to being a highly conductive organization. The approach we outline in this chapter covers the many components needed to move an organization in synch with its customers. Tools developed to help organizations analyze customer needs, such as Armstrong's Customer Dialer or ValueNet Works™, are examples of ways that a conductive organization can calibrate its strategy, culture, structure, and systems to its customers.

The ability to so closely calibrate relies on establishing high-quality relationships, partnering mindsets, and communication skills. The need to practice internally what you apply externally helps hone capabilities and improve approaches as these experiences result in further growth. But the single most important element is engendering trust. The ability to establish trust in all aspects of your relationships—both internally and externally—is the foundation for enabling the knowledge flow on which you base your customer calibration.

Emerging Principles

- A traditional organization focuses on customer retention, a leading organization focuses on customer satisfaction, and an innovative or conductive organization focuses on customer success.

- The closer the supplier is to the customer, the greater propensity for value-creating innovation.

- Gapless co-experiencing with the customer will come from suspending one's mindsets as a supplier in order to truly listen to the customer.

- The relationship between the organization and its distributor networks is a significant part of each organization's structural capital.

- The ability of an organization to partner will depend in large part on its culture and the leadership that drives it.

- Customer calibration is a constant process that informs all of the organization's thinking, actions, and relationships, enabled by the quality and speed of its knowledge flows.

- Innovation results from sharing information and creating knowledge to constantly find news ways to deliver relevant, high-quality solutions to customers.

References

1. Prahalad, C.K. and V. Ramaswamy. (2000). "Co-Opting Customer Competence." *Harvard Business Review*, Jan–Feb, pp. 79–87.
2. As above.
3. To learn more about the variations and use of this tool, visit Armstrong's extranet at http://www.armstrongpumps.com/dialer/designbuild/design_build.html
4. To learn more about Verna Allee's approach to mapping value networks, see http://www.alleetoolkit.com.

5

The Strategy-Making Perspective of the Conductive Organization

Introduction

The first key organizational capability to be considered in building a highly conductive organization is strategy (see Figure 5.1). Achieving breakthrough performance depends, in large part, on the extent to which the strategies and the business activities that flow from these strategies are responding to what's actually happening in the marketplace. Strategy is the foundation or lead organizational capability to which all other capabilities align.

We define *strategy* as the amalgamation of an organization's objectives, including the broader goals and the actions necessary to accomplish them. Strategies outline the long and short-term business objectives that cascade throughout the organization—not just the overarching business imperatives for the organization as a whole. The underlying organizational capability is *strategy making*, which entails the constant renewal of strategies based on the trends both inside and outside the organization that affect its performance.

Conductivity fuels the constant flow of new knowledge to keep strategies calibrated to the customer. If strategies no longer reflect the reality of the marketplace, they soon become obsolete. It doesn't matter how solid the other organizational capabilities are—performance will falter if the organization's strategy is not relevant to the customer. Even if the organization has the right structure, an aligned culture, and effective business processes, it will fail if its strategies

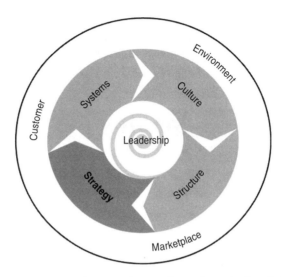

Figure 5.1   Strategy—The Foundation of Key Organizational Capabilities

are not guiding these strengths to create value in the marketplace. The weight of all other capabilities combined can't fill the void of a misguided strategy.

The Knowledge Capital Model (see Chapter 3, Figure 3.2) helps guide our thinking about strategies. Value is created when human, structural, and customer capital interact. As a result, strategies need to systematically reflect this interaction.

Strategy is essential because it's the rudder that gives coherent direction to everyone's efforts in the organization. Capabilities are assembled to realize specific objectives, based on the direction outlined by strategy.

Interdependencies Among Strategies

An organization takes its direction from a variety of strategies that we've grouped into four categories: business strategy, customer strategy, organizational strategy, and knowledge strategy. Each of these strategies is layered, dependent on each other, and symmetri-

Figure 5.2   Strategic Coherence

cal. Together they form a cohesive whole that is reflected by the business strategy (see Figure 5.2).

The overarching *business strategy* defines the organization's broad strategic intent and strategic imperatives. The *customer strategy* outlines how the organization will provide value to different segments of its customer base. It identifies the brand experience and the levels of customer relationships that are desired. The *organization strategy* addresses the core organizational capabilities required to achieve the business strategy objectives—how the organization's strategies, culture, structure, and systems will be synchronized through leadership. The *knowledge strategy* outlines the approach for increasing knowledge access and exchange, generating the new capabilities required to successfully implement strategies at all levels in order to achieve or exceed expected performance.

Strategy Making

For a highly conductive organization, strategy is much more than the final document that includes a vision, mission, objectives, and all the other requisite parts that form a comprehensive strategic plan. It's a comprehensive process that we call *strategy making*. A *strategy* is an objective, something you arrive at, a conclusion. *Strategy making* is an action, a process that you follow, a capability. When we talk about strategy as an organizational capability, we're really talking about strategy making—*the constant renewal of strategy to align and keep pace with the evolution of customer and marketplace needs.*

Strategy making includes the explicit statement of overall strategic direction, as well as its translation into objectives that cascade through all levels of the organization, including teams and individuals. In the end, everyone in the conductive organization has to be able to connect what they do to the overarching strategic intent and its supporting objectives.

Strategy making in many cases elevates the organization's strategic horizon. It uncovers new customer needs and opens up opportunities that the organization can explore. Generating capabilities needed to realize recalibrated strategies becomes a new constant that keeps the customer at the center of a highly conductive organization.

By generating strategic thinking throughout the organization, strategy making encourages people to be self-critical—to ask themselves whether what they're doing is coherent with the organization's overall strategic intent and the objectives that they've been mandated to realize. Because people throughout the organization have actively participated in shaping strategy, they've had the opportunity to gain a fuller understanding of the business context and can exercise judgement as to what information is relevant and what doesn't matter. In other words, they can increase the quality of the knowledge flow.

The conductive organization needs a level of creative abrasion throughout to ensure that the knowledge that is assimilated has been tested and proven through the collective judgement of individuals and serves as the basis for effective action.

In essence, strategy making is the capability to generate effective strategies based on our ability to accurately read the marketplace and our environment, understand our customer's needs, analyze and internalize the patterns and trends, and understand our internal strengths and weaknesses, and identify the organization's vulnerabilities. On the basis of these combined elements, we can shape the objectives that guide how we're going to realize our strategic intent and identify the capabilities that we'll need to take effective action.

Outside-In: The Customer Perspective

Developing any capability begins with the customer, and strategy is no exception. Understanding the customer's perspective, seeing the environment through the customer's eyes, is the starting point for strategy making. Being a conductive organization includes the capability to create strategies that begin with customer needs within the context of the business environment. They don't begin with what the organization *thinks* it does best, or even what it *thinks* it knows about its customers and the marketplace. If the customer isn't connected to the strategy-making process right from the beginning, then it's not going to fly.

Strategy making is a natural conduit to the customer (see Figure 5.3). With the customer as the focus of everything the conductive organization does, strategy making provides one of the primary points of connection. Given that strategy provides direction for creating value, it becomes the natural knowledge flow, the catalyst for learning with the customer and the vehicle that keeps pace with marketplace and other environmental changes.

The outside-in perspective, guided by the customer strategy, allows us to tap into customers' experiences. It informs all levels of strategy with the customer calibration that we outlined in chapter 4. For example, the organization strategy ensures that the capabilities required to achieve the business strategy objectives are available—that the culture is tuned to deliver the desired customer experience, the structures are in place to best serve the evolving requirements of the marketplace, the systems are adjusted to ensure

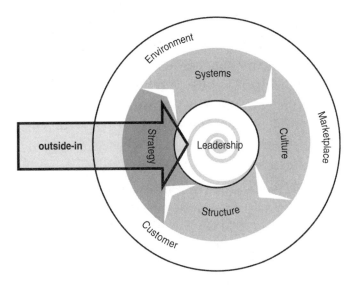

Figure 5.3 The Outside-In Perspective

seamless delivery of products and services, and leadership keeps all
the capabilities in synch.

Shared Responsibility in Strategy Making

Strategy making has to be a highly inclusive process that involves all
those who are instrumental in the realization of the strategy in an
appropriate manner. Strategy making is a cascading process in the
organization, with as much tension from the top down as from
the bottom up. By virtue of their position in the organization and
the issues they deal with, senior managers have a better perspective
to outline broad strokes of the strategy. But this has to be done
within the context of a dialogue where senior managers engage in
making meaning across the organization. Everyone must be able to
see the larger context. The bottom-up perspective brings the reality
checks and the factual observations of people who work day to day
at the customer interface. The dialogue that takes place not only val-
idates the strategic direction, but ensures a high level of ownership
on the part of all those involved.

In this environment where knowledge exchange is fluid, change management becomes less important because everyone understands the context and the rationale for what needs to happen. The conductive organization makes this exchange inherent to the way the organization functions. Whenever a new trend is perceived in the marketplace or the competition makes a new move that may change the rules of the game, anyone who sees it has the ability to bring the relevant signal to the attention of all those who need to know. A high level of conductivity in the organization is responsible for making customer-calibrated, real-time strategy making possible and first-mover advantage an outcome.

A barrier to knowledge flow occurs when the organization doesn't manage strategy making as an all-inclusive process, when it views strategy as an "us and them" division of labor. A division between "we" who create the strategy and "they" who have to make it work limits the possibilities for high-quality conductivity.

Values and Capabilities

When the values and mindsets that guide individual employees' behavior are not aligned with organizational values to create core values, conductivity is impeded and strategies are likely to fail. These unreconciled mindsets can become significant obstacles and are often at the root of the apparent inability to implement a given strategy. It's key that the organization encourages a diversity of perspectives on the business, but when the time comes to take action, it's essential that this diversity be reconciled with a course of action—something that can rally everyone with energy and commitment.

The conversations that feed the strategy-making process allow for constructive resolution of contradictory perspectives. The genuine exchange that takes place in the context of strategy making encourages people to offer differing opinions. Through this exchange, new solutions can be found—solutions that transcend the dilemmas that so often block the ability to identify important new strategic developments in organizations. These conversations also enhance the level of understanding and trust.

This form of discussion shouldn't be relegated to an annual or quarterly process. It should be an ongoing conversation that thrives on different viewpoints and strives for coherence. The exchange of information and ideas represents the foundation for the ongoing learning process that serves to fulfill the aspirations of every individual in the organization.

At a very pragmatic level, this exchange is achieved by forming teams that tackle key issues with wide participation across the organization—a process that has been used extensively at both Clarica and Armstrong.

Strategy making is a capability that gets better and better as it is applied continuously to formulate and implement more strategies over time. Recognition of patterns in the marketplace, the ability to see internal patterns, thinking situations through, and devising approaches to achieve goals are best learned in practice rather than theorizing in isolation. Team approaches to strategy building where experienced and less experienced people are brought together provide a natural forum for knowledge exchange that leads to increased capabilities. It creates the tension that challenges less valid thinking, enhances the viability of the strategy, and leads to espousing greater aspirations because of the confidence gained through the exchange of ideas.

The Strategy-Making Cycle

Developing strategy encompasses a process that goes beyond the creation of a static document that sits on a shelf and is dusted off once a year in preparation for the annual strategic planning retreat. The literature is full of books that have moved away from a focus on formulating strategy (i.e., the development process) and placed the emphasis on executing strategy. Our position is that the conductive organization has a rigorous strategy-making process that encompasses both elements—the capability to develop strategies that can be effectively implemented.

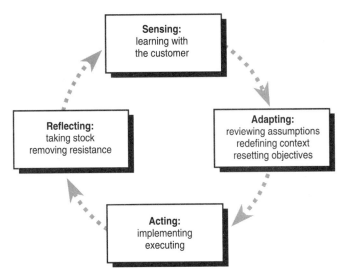

Figure 5.4 The Strategy-Making Cycle

A highly conductive organization takes a holistic view of strategy making. It's seen as an iterative, continuous process that cycles through learning with the customer from an outside-in perspective coupled with analyzing patterns and capabilities, making sense with an inward perspective. The cycle continues through experimentation, analysis, reassessment, and recalibration with customer and employee input feeding the knowledge flow at every stage (see Figure 5.4).

The constant cycling of learning and taking effective action is key to strategy making in the conductive organization. Guided by core values, fueled by new knowledge gained through learning and collaborating, the multiphased strategy-making process is in itself a generative capability. It adds a significant amount of value to the organization beyond a spiral-bound, full-color document.

Implementation

The fact that a great many strategies fail to be implemented is simply that the people who have to implement these strategies feel little ownership for them. The process of formulating strategies and their

supporting tactics must be an inclusive one that engenders ownership at all levels of the organization. Where strategies are developed
by external consultants or by senior management in isolation, and
then mandated at lower levels for implementation, there is little
chance of success.

Strategies that are developed in isolation are often deficient in the
perspective of the people who have to make them work or in understanding customer or marketplace issues; and it's a blessing that
those who have to work with strategies can actually modify them as
they're implemented. What is seen as a failure in implementation
may in fact be a failure in formulating the strategy.

Managing Risk

As we outlined in Chapter 1, a significant challenge in the transition
to a new way of doing business is managing risk. A carefully crafted
strategy that is coherent with customer needs, aligned with marketplace and environmental trends, based on capabilities, and reflective
of core values is a key mechanism for mitigating risks in a conductive organization.

With the increasing recognition of the value of intangible assets
in the knowledge era, the nature of risk has shifted. For example, a
single unethical act by an employee can cause a loss of reputation
that can result in significant business losses. Because of the connectedness of the marketplace, a seemingly small, misguided decision can take on huge proportions. Organizations run increasingly
higher risks when they have less transparency internally than what
is the norm in the marketplace. By contrast, a highly conductive
organization brings scrutiny to everyone that will foster greater
accountability across the board and ensure that no rogue practitioner undermines the organization's reputation.

Without a high degree of conductivity, the issue of governance
and the risk associated with strategic failure often culminate in difficult circumstances, where internal politics are focused on finding
scapegoats. In the end, a culture of blame and mistrust is fostered

and the probability of further strategic failure is increased. Organizations that experience failed strategies have little or no calibration with the customer. They cannot regenerate through learning. The next initiative is injected into the organization where it's typically received with cynicism, lip service, and further mistrust.

A highly conductive organization by definition will have a high degree of transparency. The framework we outline for required organizational capabilities is intended to provide a mechanism for increasing transparency, where strategies that don't gain ground are part of a continuous learning cycle—where strategies evolve with purpose. In turn, individuals and organizations become more conductive, less blaming, and more open to learning. Organizations become more porous to the outside world's view with a climate as well as the avenues in place to question behavior in a public way. There's a constant tension between available information and widespread opportunity to exercise mutual accountability.

Strategic Capabilities

Strategies identify, in turn, another type of capability that we call *strategic capabilities*. These capabilities, both individual and organizational, are elevated to a *strategic* level because they are specifically needed to realize identified business strategies.

Strategic capabilities often evolve over time in an organization and may even go unnoticed or unarticulated until they are developed to such a degree that they become obvious embedded capabilities. In other instances, strategic capabilities have been articulated as being required to meet evolving customer needs and are linked with the strategic imperatives included in all levels of strategy—business, customer, organization, and knowledge.

At Armstrong, we've identified four key strategic capabilities: mass configuration, customer relationship management, partnering in supply chains, and cost management in manufacturing. For example, mass configuration is strategic because we have the ability to build a total of 10 million end product configurations from com-

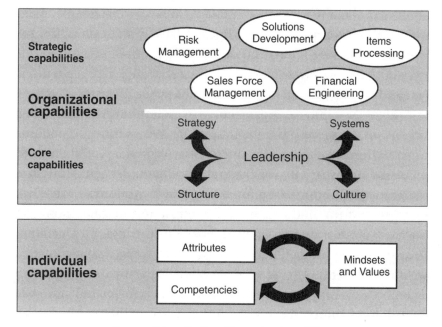

Figure 5.5   Clarica's Strategic Capabilities

ponents available in-house and ship a customized solution within weeks. Within this strategic capability is another significant factor that distinguishes us in the marketplace—the ability to work as a team and involve many different parts of the organization, working in harmony to produce the customer solution.

The process of identifying strategic capabilities is based on the ability to recognize what capabilities distinguish the organization in the marketplace. Figure 5.5 is a map of Clarica's strategic capabilities that builds on elements of individual capabilities and organizational capabilities to identify the strategic capabilities of risk management, solutions development, items processing, financial engineering, and sales force management.

Strategic Symmetry

Strategic symmetry ensures that there's alignment not only of strategies, but also of organizational and individual capabilities to the developed strategies. Analyzing strategic symmetry ensures that the organization recognizes what capabilities it needs to implement strategy. By providing coherence, a knowledge strategy is instrumental in creating strategic symmetry. It ensures that conductivity enables cascading from the overarching business strategy through the organization to individual employee plans for generating the required capabilities to meet strategic objectives.

This level of symmetry is almost holographic. Think of a hologram as an image that creates a three-dimensional form; when viewed from any angle, corner, or piece, the entire image is seen from a new perspective. Strategic symmetry is like this—each part of the organization has a view of the whole strategy and understands its context. As a result of this comprehensive, multifaceted view, the organization's leaders can afford to delegate accountability and responsibility to all parts of the organization with less risk to strategic performance.

Gaining strategic symmetry provides the necessary conditions for quality conversations that fuel the strategy-making process by which, in turn, the organization evolves. Without a holographic view and strategic symmetry, leadership remains concentrated in a few people, delegation of responsibility is inconsistently applied, and conductivity is severely inhibited.

Armstrong and Clarica Strategy-Making Approaches

As part of Armstrong's transition to calibrating the organization more closely with customer clusters, we adopted a new approach to strategy making—a process that evolved through a number of different forms. Initially, strategy was set by the top management team and deployed both functionally and cross-functionally. In the process of implementing strategic initiatives, it became clear that the organization had to work at deeper levels vertically as well as ensure that the interdependencies needed horizontally to achieve our goals were in place. When a strategy was developed by a narrow group of senior managers, it resulted in a lack of coherence, a disconnect with parts of the organization. In the end managers were required to spend an inordinate amount of time setting the context and establishing priorities to guide people's daily work.

As we increased our strategy-making capabilities, rather than having only a few of the top managers participate in the strategy sessions, we engaged about 10% of the organization. We expanded the sessions to three days to include enough time for the strategy development work as well as designing ways to make the strategy more meaningful to the entire organization. Following these strategy sessions, the outcomes were communicated to the rest of the organization by pairs of session participants.

To take the strategy to the next level of weaving components into each group's business plans, strategy session participants were broken into teams responsible for single strategic initiatives. These teams then worked with others employees to create detailed plans, that once implemented, were reviewed twice a month to ensure the initiatives were synchronized with one another and the rest of the organization.

In 2000, the emergence of virtual private networks (VPNs) as an economic IT delivery backbone changed the strategy-making dialogue at Armstrong. Prior to VPN availability, we'd been developing a common technology system for all of our operations to support our global initiatives. With the advent of VPNs, it became possible not only to have common processes and systems, but to connect these systems in such a way as to provide a single seamless approach to conductivity internally as well as to the customer. Recognizing the significance of this new capability, the strategy-making dialogues evolved from a focus on IT connectedness to the delivery of new products and services that customers identified through Customer Dialer sessions.

The plug-and-play IT architecture that we had been developing could now connect us in real time to our customers and partners in value-creation networks. The customer service capability of the organization was also significantly elevated. With leadership providing the necessary synchronization of the organizational capabilities, this technology helped drive more collaborative work inside the organization, with work groups from various operations jointly delivering new capabilities to the customer.

These groups also recognized that new skills were required to develop a deeper understanding of our value proposition from the customer's perspective. The Customer Dialer evolved from this need for better understanding—not just for our sales force, but grew to involve most people in the organization. We didn't purposefully set out on an organizational change effort. Instead, the strategies and corresponding capabilities grew out of conversations with our customers based on a heightened awareness of the strategic context of the business.

Clarica also adopted a new approach to its former once-a-year ritual of strategy development. As part of the restructuring prior to demutualization, we implemented a rigorous planning process and paid a great deal of attention to the structure. We held quarterly a two-day session with the executive committee to review our various strategy themes and talk about whether we were on the right track. These sessions were often facilitated by external resources.

Starting with information that had been gathered from our customer conversations and market intelligence, we reviewed our previous assumptions to see if they corresponded to fact. We looked at the evolution of our approach and suggested new courses of action that were often experimental.

Strategic themes identified by the executive team were then validated and fleshed out by a wider leadership group of the top 60 or 70 managers. The results were used as the basis for a 90-day planning cycle at the unit, department, and individual level. This approach ensured that strategy was constantly renewed, revitalized with customer input. Ownership cascaded throughout all layers of the organization and integrated with organizational systems and structures such as performance reviews and compensation plans.

Over time, we became much better at having productive conversations that helped us create a deeper understanding of our clients and our marketplaces and improved our capability of strategy making.

In both Armstrong and Clarica, our strategy-making approaches evolved over time and our capabilities increased with each new development. As well, individual strategy-making capabilities became widely spread as we engaged more people in continuous strategy-making activities. Strategy is no longer the property of a select few. Through the strategy-making process, the strategic intent at the highest level cascades to individual plans that create a more cohesive organization, resulting in a higher level of conductivity.

A Closer Look at the Knowledge Strategy

We move from the strategy-making process (strategy as verb) to talking in further detail about a key strategy in a highly conductive organization—the knowledge strategy.

The knowledge strategy puts in place the mechanisms that provide for accessing and exchanging knowledge. It also enables the development of generative capabilities (e.g., learning, collaborating, and strategy making). By providing for greater connectivity across the organization, a well-formulated and -implemented knowledge strategy builds coherence and increases speed and the overall agility of the organization. The knowledge strategy, which is an inherent part of the overall business strategy, becomes the basis for constant renewal and alignment with the reality of the marketplace.

Purpose

The goal of a knowledge strategy is to accelerate the development of individual and organizational capability—to increase the level of conductivity. The unimpeded flow of knowledge ensures that the core elements of organizational capability (i.e., strategy, culture, structure, systems) are dynamically adjusted to meet the challenges of the marketplace. And leadership can easily be rapidly exercised to constantly synchronize the organization to what needs to happen in order to meet the needs of customers and the challenges presented by the external environment.

A highly conductive organization is one that successfully applies a higher level of quality and broad-based engagement of its resources in pursuit of unimpeded knowledge flows. It leverages and expands the organization's general or overarching business strategy, creating opportunities for its strategic horizon that could not have been articulated without insights gained from its new knowledge. With elevated conductivity comes the opportunity for greater customer impact and breakthrough performance.

The purpose of the knowledge strategy is to provide direction for learning with the customer, utilizing the knowledge held by people throughout the organization, and leveraging the organization's substantial investment in technology. The knowledge strategy builds into the organization the mechanisms to learn as people and teams encounter issues and challenges. Learning is no longer a discrete process. It's fully embedded in the way the organization functions. As we used to say at Clarica, "Working is learning and learning is working."

Components

The knowledge strategy outlines a systematic approach to creating and harvesting the organization's knowledge to reach a higher level of conductivity. The intent is to place the organization's best knowledge (the quality dimension of knowledge flow) at the fingertips of everyone in the organization (the speed dimension of knowledge flow). It has to have a broad base and be embedded in how the organization works and creates value for its stakeholders and customers.

Three main components constitute a knowledge strategy: *culture* as the foundation, *knowledge architecture* as the blueprint of approaches, and *technology* as the enabler.

Culture. The strategy's foundation is formed by a culture and set of leadership principles. A culture that embraces self-initiation and values partnerships and interdependence supports a knowledge strategy where people are convinced that their own success is tied to the success of the organization as a whole. The alignment of individual and organizational values is essential to ensure that individual learning contributes to building organizational capability. Nurturing the level of trust and establishing quality relationships necessary to create and exchange knowledge across boundaries are key to achieving the level of conductivity required in this type of culture.

Knowledge Architecture: The blueprint for achieving the strategy's goals is explicitly outlined. Knowledge access, the ability to codify, store, retrieve, and display relevant knowledge in the course of doing work, brings the wealth of the organization's knowledge stocks to all employees and customers. Knowledge exchange facilitates sharing tacit knowledge, often in real time within virtual meeting spaces. Tapping into the organization's intangible assets exponentially increases the organization's capability to form relevant strategy, make the right decisions, and stay with the customer instead of lagging behind.

Technology infrastructure: Technology functions as the conduit for the knowledge network. To achieve the goal of having the organization's knowledge at the fingertips of all employees, as well as extended to the customer, requires the support of technology. Technology's key role is to convey information in a manner that allows individuals and teams to translate it into knowledge to take effective action. They do this by interacting with one another, internalizing the meaning, and gearing their tactics accordingly. Knowledge strategy requirements must be coordinated with the design of the technology infrastructure and the acquisition or development of new applications. The technology platform supports applications that harvest and store knowledge. It provides access to knowledge at the lowest possible transaction cost in terms of user time and effort. And finally, it enhances efficiencies by allowing for the reuse of knowledge objects.

Within the knowledge strategy, the knowledge architecture produces a blueprint of tools and approaches for creating, storing, and exchanging knowledge that is made available to the organization, utilized by a self-initiated culture, and enabled by an integrated technology platform.

Creating Knowledge Strategies

We've used a variety of approaches to create knowledge strategies in our organizations, but the place we typically start is looking at the strategic drivers of the business. It's a good place to start your thinking because it already has the customer view embedded and starts to create alignment right from the beginning. Looking at the strategic drivers, we can then see what outcomes are desired—the ends directly related to the heart of the organization's purpose. From the outcomes, we can identify the objectives and the tactics or activities needed to accomplish those objectives. Mapping the strategy's elements assures that it's comprehensive in its coverage, congruent in its approach, and aligned with the overarching business strategy (see Table 5.1).

What's missing in this table is the network of lines that connect the components across the columns. There's not a one-on-one, linear correlation between elements. Instead, there are linkages throughout that deepen the interdependence that facilitates maximum connectivity.

Conclusion

Strategy development has been the subject of countless books, articles, seminars, workshops, and courses. It's not our intention to write the definitive guide on how to create strategy in the knowledge era. Rather, our purpose is to emphasize that *strategy making*, as a comprehensive process that cycles between the organization and the customer, is a foundational organizational capability in a highly conductive organization. It's a conduit to the customer, a touch point for conversations that bring an outside-in perspective to planning.

Table 5.1 Mapping of Strategic Goals in a Knowledge Strategy

Strategic Drivers	Outcomes	Objectives	Activities
—Build leadership in product development —Build first-mover advantage in key segments —Foster a culture that demands excellence	—Provide the platform for focused integration (across sites and functions) —Provide the ability to rapidly respond to emerging opportunities —Enhance capability to partner internally and externally —Accelerate capability development in strategic areas —Accelerate work flows and decision making —Enhance innovation —Improve cost efficiency	—Provide ready access to the organization's knowledge —Build memory and knowledge continuity —Enhance retention levels —Reduce the number of "push" emails —Reduce the amount of time searching for information —Build readiness in the culture for greater conductivity	—Develop communities of practice for strategic competencies —Provide tools and processes for virtual collaboration —Develop an intranet with extensive search capabilities —Systematically develop and make accessible lessons learned —Put in place a new definition of the manager role

Strategy making has an intimate connection with the other three key organizational capabilities that generate a high level of conductivity. While there is coherence among the four, there also needs to be a slight disequilibrium. There needs to be a dynamic that triggers the recalibration. Leadership plays this role by requiring constant strategy review and renewal.

We want to limit the use of strategy as a noun and focus on it as a verb—as *strategy making*. With this new perspective, we have the foundation in place on which to shape culture, create structures, and design systems that tie strategy to the customer and put into practice the capabilities that leverage our collective customer and employee knowledge.

Emerging Principles

- It doesn't matter how solid the other organizational capabilities are—performance will falter if the organization's strategy is not relevant to the customer.

- The weight of all other capabilities combined can't fill the void of a misguided strategy.

- A strategy is an objective, something you arrive at, a conclusion. Strategy making is an action, a process that you follow, a capability.

- Generating capabilities to realize recalibrated strategies is a new constant that keeps the customer at the center of a highly conductive organization.

- The quality of knowledge flow in the organization can be improved by engaging people in conversations geared to develop a better understanding of the business's strategic context.

- People can increase the quality of knowledge flow in the organization by understanding the strategic context of the business.

- Developing any capability begins with the customer, and strategy is no exception.

- A high level of conductivity in the organization makes real-time, customer-calibrated strategy making possible and first-mover advantage an outcome.

- The multiphased strategy making process is in itself a generative capability.

- The constant cycle of learning and taking effective action is key to strategy making in the conductive organization.

- What is seen as failure in strategy implementation may in fact be a failure in formulating the strategy in the first place.

- Building strategy making as a capability will elevate the organization's strategic horizon.

- Strategic symmetry ensures that all strategies are aligned and that the required organizational and individual capabilities to realize these strategies are also aligned.

- Without strategic symmetry, leadership remains concentrated in a few, delegation of responsibility is inconsistently applied, and conductivity is severely inhibited.

- By aligning employee and customer mindsets, the strategy-making process can align organizational capabilities with marketplace requirements.

- Working is learning and learning is working in a conductive organization.

6

External and Internal Branding: The Character of the Conductive Organization

Introduction

One of our central propositions is that it is critically important to forge deep and mutually beneficial relationships between the organization and the customers it serves. These relationships should be based on new types of conversations. By permeating these relationships with conversation, a conductive organization creates the environment in which customer calibration is routinely practiced.

This chapter describes our experiences of permeating the customer-employee relationship with a textural, experiential, and aspirational congruence so that deep, trusting, and lasting relationships can be formed. Forging these relationships requires the overlay of a well-defined corporate brand—a brand that has meaning to customers and employees alike. The brand becomes a mechanism for facilitating new conversations among the conductive organization, its employees, and its customers.

In many markets today, customers do not just buy a product. They are more interested in purchasing a solution that creates an experience that is congruent with the values they hold. We see this behavior in buying decisions ranging from an organization sourcing complex IT solutions from a supplier who claims a relaxed and open culture similar to their own, to a consumer buying products from a supermarket that emphasizes its commitment to environmental causes.

Although in both cases the quality of the offering is still extremely important (the environment-friendly products must still be fit-for-purpose and the IT solution still has to address a business imperative), in a world where choice is abundant, such experiential-aspirational alignment is increasingly becoming a competitive differentiator. Consider the Body Shop example in Chapter 2. Realizing this alignment is much more than a problem for the marketing department. A supermarket chain proclaiming environmental sensitivities will quickly be discredited if customers do not see the stores practicing conservation efforts.

As well as annoying and alienating customers, such dishonesty will irritate an organization's employees. Job-seeking individuals are increasingly gravitating towards corporations that share their own values and aspirations. Continuing with the supermarket example, if employees are lured by the 'environmental' stance of the employer and then find it is not actually practiced, their likely response is to either disengage from the company (i.e., continue working for the organization but with little or no enthusiasm or interest) or leave the corporation (probably to join a competitor) at the first opportunity. This type of misalignment derails any attempt to build conductivity.

The Brand Promise

In short, an organization should take care to brand itself in ways that are honest and accurate and that resonate with the values and desired experiences of customers and employees alike. The brand represents no less than a promise of how both groups will experience the organization. Within the brand promise, the aspirations of the organization itself converge and coalesce with those of its customers and employees. The brand promise is the area where the external customer experience and internal employee experience coalesce, where employee-customer relationships, organizational capital, and customer capital are created or destroyed.

At Clarica, a brand promise of *clarity through dialogue* was developed after a great deal of research was conducted to understand the values and aspirations of both employees and customers. This tagline was a promise that Clarica would provide clear, uncomplicated information and would be accessible to talk with its customers. The brand promise is supported internally with dedicated resources—people who champion the use of plain language in all forms of communication based in a consulting practice and the opportunity for all employees to increase their written and verbal communication skills using e-learning modules residing on the intranet.

In simple terms, Clarica has fulfilled its brand promise by putting into practice the most important principle of corporate branding—an organization can only apply externally to its customers and partners what it practices internally with its employees. Like customers, employees who see a disconnect between the brand promise and the brand experience lose trust in the organization. Without this congruence, the brand will be unsustainable, relationships will atrophy, and the organization's customer and human capital will be eroded if not destroyed.

The Character of the Organization

In this approach to branding, the brand promise along with the employee and customer experiences that correspond to that brand can collectively be described as the *character of the firm* (see Figure 6.1). This figure is largely based on the work of Jasper Kunde. (1) We find this a useful description as it suggests that how we define an organization in the knowledge era has to be as much about the values of the customer as about those of the organization. This idea resonates with the requirement to take an outside-in/inside-out view of the organization—the requirement to learn at the customer interface and bring that new knowledge for interpretation and action.

The brand promise represents the link between the employee experience and customer experience. It's based on the premise that employees can't possibly provide a customer experience that is con-

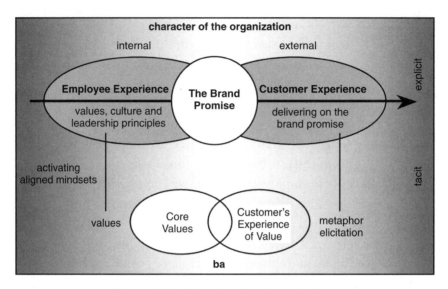

Figure 6.1 Character of an Organization

trary to the experience they live within the organization. For instance, employees in a call center can't be asked to care for the customer with a strong sense of ownership if they themselves find that they're neither respected by their managers nor are their needs taken into account in their place of work. In other words, the experience employees are meant to provide to customers must be akin to the experience they themselves have within the organization.

The brand promise is positioned at the overlap between the customer's experience of value and the core values of the organization and its employees. At Clarica, we discovered that employees had values that caused them to be attentive to customers. It was easy to match this employee value to customers' needs. Customers wanted communications that were clear, that increased their understanding of the long-term financial solutions they were purchasing. One of the key issues expressed by customers in relating to an insurance company was that they had to buy solutions they didn't fully understand. They wanted to obtain more knowledge about these solutions every time they interacted with the company. We focused our efforts on this need because we knew that we could meet this requirement better than our competitors—our employees were capable of providing customers with more knowledge about solutions. In other words, our customers' needs (i.e., what they saw as valuable) overlapped with our employees' values—a commitment to our brand promise of providing clarity through dialogue.

Subsequent research showed that by satisfying this need, customers who dealt with Clarica not only gave high value to this dimension of their experience, they also increased their expectations in this regard. To a large extent, the brand was shaping the marketplace around a promise that resonated with customers and that was aligned to a highly credible solution delivery because it fit the natural inclination of our employees. And our employees themselves became more demanding in their experience of *clarity through dialogue* within the organization. This was a challenge we welcomed because we knew that our efforts were creating a strong advantage for us in the marketplace. We were staking a claim that our competitors could only aspire to.

The ideal customer experience with the brand promise is best defined by analyzing the cause-effect chain that underlies the perception of value. Our research showed us how customers recognized whether or not we were living the brand—whether or not we were providing them with the brand's promised experience no matter what access point they used to interact with the company. The employee experience, on the other hand, was affected by how leadership principles were applied in the organization—how these principles interacted with the culture. Leadership behavior shaped the employees' experience.

It was also clear to us that the customer experience was a direct outcome of the leadership principles enacted within the organization. The close relationships created with customers through the brand promise stemmed from the overlap between the values lived in the organization and expectations of its customers. This overlapping space is what Nonaka and Takeuchi (2) describe as *ba* in their groundbreaking work on knowledge and innovation. This connection is created by the brand promise at a tacit level. At the explicit level, the brand promise lived through the employee and customer experience makes the character of the organization more tangible to everyone.

What is Branding?

In general, corporate brands:

- Purposefully create a desired image of the organization for both customers and employees. This responsibility is shared equally across the organization, not just within the marketing and communications departments.
- Describe the compelling value proposition that is inherent to the customer experience first, and then to the employees.
- Are clear as to what is unique and distinctive about the organization for both employees and customers.
- Are authentic and grounded in reality, but are at the same time aspirational.
- Make a commitment that has credibility, yet has to be realized.
- Build coherence. An organization cannot sustain delivery of a customer experience that is incongruent with the experience of its employees.

External Branding

Let's first consider branding as a customer experience. By understanding the experience required by the customer, we can begin to create the organizational capabilities to deliver solutions based on customer needs. Once we articulate the brand promise, it's communicated broadly both internally and externally to our customers, employees, and value-creation network partners.

The brand is a perception that the customer has of an organization. The customer's perception has a lot to do with the values the customer holds as an individual. The customer experience encompasses the many ways (emotional, cognitive, social, and functional) that he or she comes into contact with the facets of the organization's brand.

A successful brand enables customers to connect to the organization. How customers use the product or service solution indicates who they want to be. The relationship they form extends their values and their sense of self-worth.

Harley-Davidson

Consider the brand promise of a Harley-Davidson motorcycle. What is it about this bike that compels its purchase by people from across generations, across continents, and across social classes? What is it about the product that has led to the creation of The Harley Owners Group®, which boasts a global membership of 750,000 people who are united by a common passion—a commitment to "making the Harley-Davidson dream a way of life?" (3)

There is clearly something about this brand that resonates deep within the psyche of many people. What's more, it's not uncommon for Harley-Davidson employees to be just as passionate about the product, nor is it unusual for employees to have a tattoo of the bike somewhere on their bodies! As with Harley-Davidson, the brand should enable customers to realize their aspirations and yearnings, irrespective of whether they are explicitly articulated or implicitly perceived.

Clarica Example

In 1997, The Mutual Group, as Clarica was then called, was going through a process of demutualization to become a publicly listed corporation after 120 years of mutual ownership. As part of this transformation, The Mutual Group's leadership team chose to understand its historic values and make explicit the culture of the corporation. They did this in order to ensure that the new organization would build on the platform of its long-standing success and retain its strong customer relationships.

Customer Research

The organization involved customers, through focus groups, surveys, and other instruments, to articulate The Mutual Group's culture. They sought to discover what customers felt was a satisfying customer experience. The Mutual Group's leadership believed that it was through its relationships with its customers that sustainable financial success would be achieved.

Research showed that a satisfying customer experience could be described in two words—trust and clarity. As part of that research, customers were asked to rank the qualities of their agents. Further analysis showed that customers who ranked their agents highest on trust and clarity shared the following qualities that distinguished them from customers who ranked agents highest on other characteristics. These customers:

- Had purchased other Mutual Group products in addition to life insurance.
- Were considerably more likely to purchase other products in the future.
- Were more likely to provide their agent with referrals and were much more likely to refer other individuals to their agent on their own.
- Were much more likely to continue to purchase life insurance in the future from their agent than through other channels (e.g., banks).
- Were less likely to switch agents or go to another insurance provider.

At this time of dramatic change, the organization also had evidence that The Mutual Group was, in the minds of the majority of the public, largely undifferentiated from its competitors. This was not surprising given that little differentiation existed at that time in the financial services sector. So The Mutual Group recognized that competitive advantage could be achieved by developing and enhancing relationships and capabilities focused on clarity and trust. Their strategy included creating a strong brand promise and experience.

Mapping the Customer Experience

To confirm the importance of clarity and trust as key values, Clarica carried out customer interviews to map cause and effect chains. They identified what customers wanted from their relationships with employees and agents—what solutions they wished to secure or what aspiration they wished to satisfy.

Clarica's research with customers revealed in concrete terms what experience they wanted from their chosen provider of long-term financial services. Customers wanted trust-based conversations that gave them expert advice explained in a simple, clear way. Their aspirations were articulated in ways that were useful to give more relevance to the brand in the minds of Clarica's customers. Customers were saying, "I *want* to be in control of my future. I *will* be in control of my future if people have given me all the information that I need and if I understand the financial solutions I am choosing. The more information they give me, the more trust I have in them. The more trust I have, the better I can meet the needs of my family because I am in control of my financial future." These were extremely useful findings to position and leverage the brand.

To measure the branding strategy's success, which included advertising campaigns aimed at heightening awareness of its new name and the *clarity through dialogue* promise, Clarica surveyed Canadian residents in early 2000. A substantial majority of Canadians were shown to recognize the Clarica name and a surprisingly large proportion of them declared that they would actively consider purchasing a product from Clarica. Another measure of success was that the Clarica brand was valued at over 10 times the investment in creating and communicating the brand. By that time, branding had become entrenched as the connector between Clarica's culture and its customers.

Mapping Customer Values to Employee Values

Clarica already knew through the analysis of its culture and values that its employees had a strong predilection for talking to the customer, caring a great deal about the customer, and genuinely helping the customer understand how the solutions the organization was providing would help the customer reach his or her aspirations.

It was clear that Clarica could gain a competitive advantage by continuing to do what it had historically been good at—caring for and communicating clearly with the customer.

With demutualization, the renaming of the corporation was crucial. *Clarica* essentially means *clarity through dialogue.* Conversations are not the only means by which trust can be engendered, but the name and logo clearly suggest the two-way flow of information and knowledge that is critical in the conductive organization. This corporate renaming clearly signalled that the brand promise would be the central focus of the organization, its employees, and its agents.

When there is convergence between the employees' and the organization's values, the brand promise closely maps to the customer experience. When customers, employees, and the organization all share the same vision, quality relationships are easier to forge and knowledge has a better chance of flowing unimpeded.

The ZMET Technique

To further map customers' relationships with agents and paint a fuller picture of what the customer perceived as a satisfying experience, Clarica applied an approach called ZMET (Zaltman Metaphor Elicitation Technique) invented by Harvard University Professor Jerry Zaltman. (4)

ZMET is a method of uncovering the mental models that guide customer thinking and behavior. Drawing from cognitive science, the approach recognizes that human beings mainly think in images, not words. So instead of using text-based surveys, customers are asked to paint a picture of their emotional relationship with an organization, its products or services, using collage and photographs.

One customer portrayed his relationship with Clarica and his experience with the Clarica brand several years after Clarica had launched its brand strategy. His collage showed the substantial progress the organization had made in distinguishing itself in the marketplace. To depict insurance companies in general, he chose a group of penguins overlaying a skyscraper to show that it was difficult if not impossible to tell one from another—they were all part of the corporate world, offering more or less the same products and services. His second picture showed that, after he established a relationship with a Clarica agent, that agent was now distinct from the group and had been invited into his private world. The collage included a person lounging on a couch, enjoying a bottle of wine, soccer ball at his feet, and a penguin sharing his space.

The Nestlé Experience with ZMET

The research Zaltman completed with Nestlé shows how this image-oriented technique can elicit a deeper understanding of the connections between a customer and a branded product—the Nestlé Crunch candy bar. (5) When he used ZMET to probe the attitudes of ten Nestlé Crunch fans, Zaltman first uncovered what you might expect. Through their pictures and Photoshop collages, subjects revealed that they saw the candy bar as a small indulgence in a busy world, a source of quick energy, and something that just tasted good.

But as Zaltman probed more deeply, he unearthed a surprise. The Nestlé Crunch candy bar turned out to be a very powerful icon of time—something the company had never imagined. The research participants brought in pictures of old pickup trucks, children playing on picket-fenced suburban lawns, grandfather clocks, snowmen, and American flags. The candy bar evoked memories of childhood, of simpler times. It was less a workday pick-me-up than a time machine back to perhaps happier days. Gaining this insight suggested a different relationship between the company and its customers and a different direction for future advertising campaigns.

Branding and Values

The brand must be inextricably linked to the values of the organization. An effective brand hinges on the fundamental connection between the organization's collective values and customer experience. When the needs, aspirations, values, and capabilities of customers coincide with those of employees, the organization achieves the complementarity that all organizations seek to establish between themselves and their customers.

Branding not only embodies values that give prominence to creating and sustaining an appropriate customer experience, but also requires that individuals throughout the organization actually use these values as the fulcrum for decision making. Effective branding is the external manifestation of the values of the organization. Translating those values into a promise, the organization makes a commitment to the customer that says, when you deal with us, this is what you will experience. If there is a breakdown in that experience, there is a foundation in place to repair it because common principles have been identified.

Clarica Agent Interviews

Returning to the Clarica experience, an independent exercise to map how agents viewed their relationship with both Clarica and their customers produced findings remarkably similar to the customer maps. Agents wished to possess good knowledge of the customer and to engage in trusting solution-focused conversations. The perceptions of agents corresponded closely to what customers had revealed.

Mapping the Clarica Employee Experience

Finally, by understanding the values and motivators of its employees, Clarica could see that employees sought knowledge to enable them to engage in trust-based dialogues. They wanted to increase their capabilities and knowledge in order to enhance their employability and provide for their own families. The aspirations of the employees were aligned to those of the agents and the customers.

Brand Congruence

By pinpointing aspirational congruence among customers, agents, and employees, it became possible to explain that stakeholders also shared common goals and would benefit enormously from forging deep trust-based relationships. Clarica was able to configure the brand promise of clarity through dialogue as a practical relationship and capability-building tool.

Customers clearly stated that they wanted information to be explained to them. Agents and employees stated that they wanted knowledge. Based on these needs, structures and processes had to be established for gaining access to this knowledge. Knowledgeable employees help create knowledgeable agents who can provide information for customers to become knowledgeable as well. The aligned values were instrumental in enabling knowledge flows.

Customers and employees also indicated that they wanted to be treated with care. Agents stated that they perceived caring as a critical characteristic in how they related to customers. To provide a caring approach to the way it did business, Clarica turned to one of its core values, partnership, to describe how agents and employees were expected to interact with customers and each other. Partnership had to do with building sustainable high-quality relationships based on dignity, understanding, and respect.

Branding at Armstrong

The branding approach at Armstrong continues to evolve as we align our core values and create congruence between the customer and employee brand experiences. Our 70-year history is reflected in our purpose, which was created and subsequently validated by two generations of family management. Now with the third generation managing the company, we rearticulated our purpose and values by engaging our entire organization in a dialogue about our business practices. In this exchange, employees were able to articulate how we could improve our processes and approaches to provide better connections internally for sharing experiences and externally to gain a deeper understanding of our customers.

As a result of our initial work, we developed a survey of customer needs and expectations, using internal resources to map the served and unserved marketplace needs. This quantitative research was augmented with a qualitative inquiry into the customer experience to extract the essential concerns of our customer clusters. The results of the two research initiatives pointed to three core elements of a brand intent: learn, collaborate, and make it happen. At the time, we didn't see the connection between learning and collaborating—that they were two key generative capabilities. However, through additional organization-wide workshops, the essential elements of the brand theme were endorsed.

Much of the early brand work was completed at the same time that we were focusing on customer calibration and developing the Customer Dialer. We were simultaneously working inside and outside the organization, getting a better understanding of the company from employee and customer perspectives while looking for congruence in their comments.

Before launching the brand to the customer community, we undertook an industry benchmarking exercise to assess the long-term impact of our branding efforts. We used a multiscale survey that provided a baseline for the health of the brand and validated our brand proposition.

As we continue in our work, we've identified four elements to reflect the brand promise: Community, Innovation, Service joined by our belief that *we are stronger together*. Customers and employees want to receive and provide a high level of service quality. By working together in an open and genuine way, we can innovate together and provide each other with a more compelling and sustainable future.

To further explain the brand promise, we've created the tag line: *Armstrong: experience building. . . .* As an open-ended statement, we're inviting our customers to complete it with a phrase that defines what they want to build. It's intended to be a compelling offer to develop new capabilities with our customers and stakeholders and deepen the value-adding relationship that results.

Our recent brand work has focused on operationalizing our internal values and brand efforts with our customers and external partners. We've been working to synchronize our customer strategy with structures, systems, and our brand articulation.

The customer strategy focuses on each customer cluster in our value network. The organizational structures needed to realize these strategies are in place. At the same time, the enabling IT infrastructure has been enhanced to deliver self-service capability to the customers for order inquiries as well as for technical information and assistance 24 hours a day, seven days a week. Additional systems, processes, and supply chain enhancements improved product delivery by 300%, making it the best in the industry.

Connecting the organizational values with the customer brought the brand and customer strategies to life and energized the delivery of enhanced services to our specific customer segments.

Conclusion

Delivering on a brand promise by providing a brand experience to both customers and employees is another dimension of the conductive organization. Creating a character for the organization and being consistent in the delivery of the brand promise are dependent on knowledge flow—on having rich conversations, through a variety of channels, with customers and employees.

Emerging Principles

■ An authentic and effective brand is based on the trust that flows from a congruent customer and employee experience.

■ Customers are more interested in purchasing a solution that resonates with the way they wish to experience the world, that is congruent with the values they hold, and that corresponds to their aspirations. The brand becomes a mechanism for facilitating new conversations among the conductive organization, its employees, and its customers.

■ With the development of a strong brand, the aspirations of the organization are brought in line with those of its customers and employees.

■ An organization can only apply externally to its customers and partners what it practices internally with its employees.

■ The brand must be inextricably linked to the values of the organization. An effective brand hinges on the fundamental connection between the organization's collective values and customer experience. If there is a breakdown in that experience, there is a foundation in place to repair it because common principles have been identified.

References

1. Kunde, J. (2000). *Corporate Religion.* London: Pearson Education.
2. For more information on the concept of *ba*, see Nonaka, I. and H. Takeuchi. (1995). *The Knowledge-Creating Company: How Japanese Companies Create the Dynamics of Innovation.* New York: Oxford University Press and Nonaka, I. and N. Konno. (1998). "The Concept of 'Ba': Building a Foundation for Knowledge Creation." *California Management Review,* 40, (30), pp. 40–54.
3. For more information on The Harley Owners Group®, see www.harley-davidson.com.
4. For more information on ZMET see **www.hbs.edu/mml/zmet.html**.
5. Pink, D. (1998). "Metaphor Marketing." *Fast Company.* (14), pg. 214.

7

Culture: The Collective Mindsets of the Conductive Organization

Introduction

The second key organizational capability of the highly conductive organization is culture (see Figure 7.1). An organization's culture reflects the collective mindsets of its employees. It's best represented by, "That's just how things are done around here." Having a culture that is engaged in fulfilling the customer imperative relies on having employee values focused in the same direction—on the customer.

Culture is tacit and therefore more difficult to articulate and codify. As a result it's often poorly understood and rarely managed as an organizational capability. But by systematically unearthing employee values and understanding the organization's historical context, we can identify, harness, and shape culture so that it becomes an integral organizational capability for enabling high performance.

Starting with Values

Culture and values are inextricably intertwined. Culture is a reflection of values, so we should start the conversation with how values further an organization's ability to be conductive. A critical element in identifying a culture is a concerted effort to surface and make visible employee values—values that are shared organization-wide and have been developed within the organization over its history.

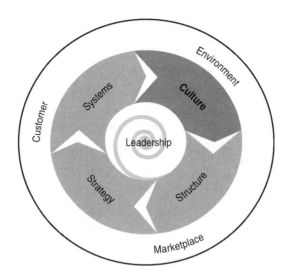

Figure 7.1   Culture—A Core Organizational Capability

Making values visible enables the leadership team to compare
employee values with the behaviors they feel are needed to implement strategy. Where gaps are found, or potentially serious resistance identified, steps can be taken to carefully develop a set of
shared values that align with strategy. Focusing on values is not
something to be undertaken because it's a feel-good thing to do. It's
a necessary building block of high performance and strategic
success.

Individual values are ideals that help us set priorities and guide
behavior. *Core values* are the values that employees and the organization hold in common. From the perspective of the conductive
organization, core values serve as the behavioral parameters that
guide how knowledge is shared and capabilities are built. When
employees recognize they share core values with the organization,
they're more likely to enter into value-creating relationships among
themselves and with customers. Most important, employees will be
more likely to commit to strategic goals.

Values and Employee Commitment

Customers are increasingly showing a preference for building rela-tionships with organizations who share their values. Employees as well are more likely to commit to an organization whose values are congruent with their own.

When the values held by an organization do not correspond to the values espoused by its employees, the results are generalized feel-ings of alienation and frustration. Employees experience dissonance in their everyday work life between their own values and those of their colleagues, and this dissonance can result in a dysfunctional organization. If individual and organizational values do not con-verge, then employees will either leave when opportunities arise or disengage from organizational goals and activities. They will not provide the energy, enthusiasm, and discretionary effort that are needed to claim and maintain a competitive advantage.

Of course, people want to be paid for their work, but they will only contribute fully to organizations out of a sense of commitment. At its core, business is really about achieving personal and organi-zational greatness. In this context, it's essential for individuals to see a connection between their values and the organization's values— without that convergence, they can't fully commit themselves to the organization's goals.

Value Priorities

Values are internalized ideals. At a fundamental level, they are pri-orities that guide us in making everyday choices and shape our behavior. A complexity of working with values, however, is that, although they serve as an internal rudder in our everyday lives, they are for the most part unvoiced and operate at the implicit level.

Without guidance very few people would be able to clearly artic-ulate the values by which they live. Consequently, both Clarica and Armstrong have deployed values-based instruments to help indi-viduals identify their values, to establish core values, and to work to align core values with the strategic behaviors required by each organization.

Aligning Individual and Corporate Values

We aren't suggesting that you impose on every employee the same set of individual values. All employees will have their own sets of values, prioritized as they see fit and individually configured. We suggest identifying a common set of core values on which employees can agree. The organization can then recognize and leverage them as its cultural characteristics. At Armstrong, we've identified learning, innovation, service, and community as our core values. They articulate an organizational mindset and reflect how we want to be perceived internally and externally.

This core set of values also allows the organization to promote diversity among individuals with confidence because it has determined the core values that employees and the organization hold in common. Outside of the core, individuals can be as diverse as they really are. We need diversity to respond to the diverse values of our customers. In fact, it is essential that the number of shared values be kept to a minimum in order to let this diversity flourish. Too many core values would suffocate the organization.

Values Initiative at Armstrong and Clarica

Armstrong's values initiative began in 1990 with renewed emphasis in 2000 during the implementation of a new organizational structure that supported two key strategies: place the customer at the center of the organization and establish a mutually reinforcing approach to leverage corporate strengths. Armstrong's senior management team concurred that this new customer-calibrated structure would only be effective if employees were able to work across departmental boundaries with a high level of collaboration and trust. They also felt a need to harmonize leadership approaches and believed that a minimal set of convergent values would provide a common reference point for navigating the changes required to achieve true customer calibration and a high level of conductivity.

Workshops held through the company asked employees to validate identified values based on their perception of behavior: Do I live the values? Does my department live the values? And, does the management live the values? In addition, people were asked their opinions on what could be done at the individual, department, and management levels to deepen the values in the organization.

Clarica's values initiative began in 1997 and was intended to coincide with the organization's demutualization, a significant change in literally everything relating to the company, including its name. Shifting from The Mutual Group to Clarica and from a customer-owned to a shareholder-owned organization had potentially massive cultural implications, with the added requirement of being shareholder-focused as well as customer-focused. Many employees feared that the organization would become "lean and nasty" overnight—a predictable response to a new corporate mandate to create shareholder value.

However, Clarica's senior executive team strongly believed that what had enabled the organization to enjoy sustainable financial success historically had to be understood and contextualized for a new era. It was felt that if the values of The Mutual Group were lost or seriously compromised in the dash to the stock market, then shareholder value would eventually be destroyed rather than created as employees and customers became increasingly alienated.

At the outset both Armstrong and Clarica decided that to infuse a high level of ownership and thereby increase the likelihood of identifying core values that would support their new strategic directions, they would involve as many people as possible in defining the core values. Concerted efforts were made to understand both the past and the present in order to inform the culture that the organizations wished to establish for the future. This future culture was guided by the strategic vision of the organization (see Figure 7.2).

This approach diverges substantially from the more common method of values identification. Typically, values are debated and ar-

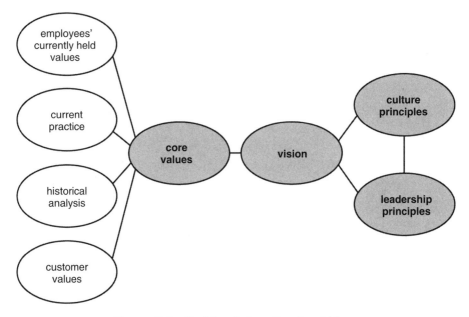

Figure 7.2   Evolving Culture Based on Values

ticulated by a small group of senior leaders and then communicated organization-wide as the "new" way of working. At best, the values are deployed throughout the organization through a series of workshops explaining to teams and individuals what the new values mean.

The values work at Clarica started with a survey of all employees to understand how their individual values compounded into strands that formed corporate values. At the same time, employees were asked to what extent the organization was actually living these values based on their experience. As a result, the survey identified not only the aggregate values of individual employees, but also measured the extent to which they perceived the organization applying these values in everyday work. A comprehensive review of Clarica's history was also undertaken to identify how corporate values have been manifested. Values were also identified in focus groups conducted with customers.

This extensive research provided a clear picture of the corporate value of the company, clearly delineating espoused values from those displayed in the way the organization actually functioned. Based on the aggregation of the corporate values, a vision of the ideal culture was developed and the leadership principles that would lead to the actualization of such a culture were formulated.

Historical Analysis

To understand its cultural history, Clarica reviewed documents dating back to the formation of the Mutual Group in the 1870s and interviewed a number of retired employees. The historical analysis showed that caring for and being of service to its customers and having its employees be supportive of their peers were values that had always been important.

Armstrong also interviewed retirees and systematically mapped the evolution of their culture and values, beginning with the presentation of a set of service values by the founder, Samuel Armstrong, to the company's sales force in 1929 (see Table 7.1). Samuel Armstrong committed his organization to create and maintain the highest quality product and to provide almost unheard-of levels of customer service. Through two changes of family leadership and the coming and going of many employees, this commitment became much more than corporate folklore. It became the understood "way we do things around here," a cultural underpinning that transcended personnel changes at any level. By making visible its cultural history, the present leadership was able to see how deeply entrenched the organization's originally espoused service values had become.

At both Armstrong and Clarica, subsequent values work with employees, customers, and partners confirmed that the core values that had historically directed organizational actions were still as powerful as they had been and just as relevant a source of competitive advantage. The values initiative became a process of rearticulating the values for today's market demands.

Table 7.1 Armstrong's Culture Timeline

Date	Actions
1929	Service values presented to sales force in Niagara Falls meetings
1934	S.A. Armstrong Limited incorporated. First use of "industrial landscape logo"
1940–1945	Wartime munitions work
1949	New plant built on O'Connor Drive to house 125 employees to better service customers and increase innovation
1950	S.A. Armstrong dies suddenly. J.A.C. Armstrong takes over family business
1965	Company starts global expansion. Armstrong Pumps Limited (APL) is incorporated in the UK
1966	Global expansion continues with incorporation of Armstrong Pumps Inc. (API) in the US
1988	Move to state-of-the-art plant on Bertrand Avenue in Toronto. Building wins architectural design awards
1990	C.A. Armstrong and J.C. Armstrong are appointed to chief operating positions. Focused factories introduced to all plants
1992	Incorporation of Armstrong Darling Inc. (ADI) in Quebec
1993	Triton ERP implemented
1994	Northwest Switchgear (UK) is purchased Purpose and values rearticulated and published
1997	Six S introduced and process improvements made
1999	Triton upgraded to Baan IV across the organization. Corporate website developed
2000	Values surveys conducted with all Armstrong employees in the UK, Canada, and US
2001	Reaffirmation of original values at Simcoe XX meeting Values surveys conducted with suppliers and customers Partnership agreement with Konverge Digital Solutions Inc. completed Alliance agreement with supplier completed I2 supply chain software implemented
2003	Brand articulation *Armstrong: Experience Building . . .*

Rather than presenting employees with an artificially developed set of new values, both organizations first identified the values that had always been of historical importance. The values that had been intrinsic to past success became the bedrock on which further cultural evolution would be based.

Deploying Values at Clarica

The senior management team concurred that the values initiative could be an effective way to clearly define what the new organization stood for and to provide its employees with a strong central image around which to coalesce. And with the financial services industry experiencing unprecedented change, there was an urgent need to highlight the organization's capabilities to cope with change and to foster employee commitment to change. The leadership team believed that this could only be achieved within a high-trust environment and that this trust could be achieved through values work. They contended that establishing core values creates a high level of trust and a foundation for commitment to partnering by both the organization and its employees.

Most important, the initiative was launched as a way to place the customer at the center of the business. Focus groups and surveys were used to capture what customers required in terms of value-added services. The values initiative was seen as a mechanism by which the organization could respond to these value-added dimensions.

Values Survey

In partnership with the US-based Values Technology (1), Clarica developed a survey to identify employee values. Distributed to 5,500 people (including all Canadian and US employees and all Canadian agents), the survey contained 125 questions. Using a multiple-choice format, employees were asked to indicate the statement that most accurately reflected their feelings at the time.

The responses were mapped against a values framework. As the questionnaires were completed, aggregate value priorities began to emerge. This information, along with the historical analysis, data from customers, and findings from workshops with the senior leaders on the values they believed the organization needed to succeed, led to the collating of three core organizational values that would be used to steer the future behavior and actions of the organization:

Partnership: building and maintaining high-quality relationships of mutual accountability based on dignity, understanding, and respect.

Stewardship: acting with integrity and accountability to maximize value, using our time, money, resources, and talent toward the understanding and service of the customer.

Innovation: sharing information and creating knowledge to constantly find new ways to deliver relevant high-quality solutions.

These core values would become the way the organization was managed on a day-to-day basis and would serve as the foundation of Clarica's partnering stewardship culture model (see Figure 7.3).

With the use of terms such as self-initiation, partnering, learning from customers, and developing capabilities, we see how culture and values coalesce to identify customer-centric behaviors and mindsets required by a conductive organization.

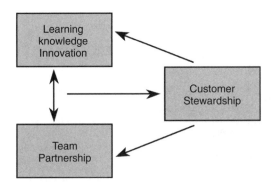

Figure 7.3 Clarica's Partnering Stewardship Model

Values and Self-Development

The values instrument also became a powerful tool for self-development. Each employee received a personal values statement, based on their survey responses that mapped their values against the core value streams. The entire process was confidential and results were electronically communicated.

This confidentiality is important for two key reasons. First, values are internalized and highly personal. They go to the core of who we are as individuals. Therefore opening up these values can be an unnerving process for the individual. It may be the first time employees have been exposed to the innermost drivers of their personalities. Very few people would be willing to do this in a public arena. Second, employees will be naturally reluctant to do this exercise if they feel that having different values from those identified as core values might exclude them from future activities or even lead to termination.

With their values identified, the employees can then create action plans to strengthen the alignment between their capabilities and required core value behaviors. At Clarica, employees were provided with the opportunity to create partnership, stewardship, and innovation action plans. For example, a behavior associated with partnership is "dialogue, listen, understand," which has corresponding values of "sharing, listening, trust," "rights, respect," and "empathy." Through an online mechanism employees at Clarica could access learning objects to help them develop these capabilities.

These action plans create organizational capabilities in that they steer employees toward living the core values. Of course, they also build individual capabilities, since skills in listening and understanding, for example, are clearly transportable and valuable in the marketplace.

Teamwork

A compelling reason for individuals to develop such skills is that, in a values-based conductive organization, the core values underpin all activities, decisions, and conversations. For example, Armstrong has a core value of community, the description of which includes the statement "we encourage trust through integrity." Consequently, trust and integrity underpin all that the organization does. Trust and integrity must not be compromised—something that all employees know.

With core values made explicit, it is much easier to assemble effective multidisciplinary teams. Each employee will already know the behavioral expectations of the team. Moreover, the sharing of the common values-based language will help ensure that meaningful connections within the team can be forged. Behavior and language congruity go a long way to creating the trusting relationships required for effective partnerships and interdependence.

Values Recap

Adherence to well-defined corporate values allows the organization to accelerate change without losing the trust of its employees. It gives the organization greater agility, which alone would be a major contribution to the effectiveness of an organization at a time when most markets are compelled by the technological innovations that surround us to move at warp speed. Placing change in the context of commitment to evolving values diminishes the friction or energy leakage inherent in change.

The identification of values creates an objective framework within which individuals and groups can test actions. Values become a lens that allows individuals within the organization to see themselves from the outside as well as from the inside. The way that values connect with each other and the discussions and debates needed to interpret and act on these connections seem to create fresh angles from which to examine the solutions to familiar problems. With a foundation in the importance of values to the conductive organization, we move to the next level of exploring culture as a key capability in the conductive organization.

Defining Culture

We introduced the chapter by saying that culture reflected the collective mindsets of the individual employees. We expand that definition to: *the sum of the individual opinions, shared mindsets, values, and norms.*

Culture is a key enabler of business performance. It can make or break strategies. Employees are the ones who must implement strategies, and they will fail (or unconsciously refuse) to do so if the strategies of the corporation, no matter how sound from a business perspective, are incongruent with the organization's culture. For example, a strategy based on customer-centricity and partnerships will be difficult to implement if the culture is task-focused and based on the power of functional silos.

Edgar Schein, Professor Emeritus at the MIT Sloan School of Management, suggests that culture consists of three components: artefacts, values and behavioral norms, and beliefs and assumptions. (2)

Artefacts: The visible, tangible, and audible characteristics of an organization that can be divided into three categories: physical, behavioral, and verbal manifestations. Physical manifestations may include the buildings and offices, internal layout, design and logos, and material objects of the organization. Behavioral manifestations can be identified by traditions and customs, ceremonies and rituals, and the communication pattern of the organization. Verbal manifestations can be found in stories, myths, jokes, anecdotes, heroes, metaphors, and jargon bandied throughout the organization.

Values and behavioral norms: The social principles, goals, and standards within a culture that define what an organization cares about form the basis for making judgements and can be referred to as an ethical or moral code. Behavioral norms are associated with values and are defined as unwritten rules that are recognized by employees of a particular group in both social and corporate cultures. Norms set boundaries and establish what behavior can be expected, or what is considered common and acceptable to employees.

Beliefs and assumptions: The core of the organization's culture, assumptions represent what employees believe to be reality and therefore influence what is perceived. They are invisible and taken for granted, existing outside of everyday awareness. Employees believe that their assumptions are the truth and are not open to question, and that they affect experiences within their cultural life.

We recognize that different employees of an organization may have divergent assumptions about how their organization works, which may result in a variety of beliefs within one company. For this reason we place significant emphasis on the identification of a shared set of core values around which individuals can coalesce.

Limitations of Cultural Change

Programs intended to change culture have been widely deployed within corporations in recent years. A 1999 survey of 236 organizations from throughout the world conducted by the UK-based Business Intelligence found that almost 60% of (mainly large) organizations had recently attempted to change their corporate culture, while almost 20% had plans to do so. (3) Organizations are clearly investing substantial resources in attempts to change their cultures.

Although we recognize the business imperatives that impel culture change initiatives, we've observed that organizations typically fail to extract lasting benefits from such efforts. Cultural change initiatives presuppose that it is possible to take an existing culture and transform it into something different by following a set program.

What these approaches fail to recognize is that organizational cultures have very deep roots that have been spreading out, unseen yet pervasively, throughout the history of that organization. Much that represents a corporate culture has been in place for longer than anyone within the organization can recall.

When shaping a culture, it can be destructive to attempt to change that culture without acknowledging with great respect and humility its historical roots. If for strategic reasons the executive team wants to change a culture from one that has historically accepted a hierarchy of decision-making processes to one in which employees are empowered to take responsibility for customer solutions, then this change is much more than a structural issue. It'll require careful unearthing of what employees value in the hierarchical structure before they will commit to the change.

It's possible that a deeply ingrained culture will not allow itself to be changed without recognizing historical forces, and, even if change is forced upon it, it will spring back to its original shape at the first opportunity.

Characteristics of a High-Performance Culture

Virtually all cultural change programs, however well the corporate leaders understand culture, are launched with the intention of creating a high-performance culture. But what does a high-performance culture look like? Our work at Clarica and Armstrong and with other organizations has helped us identify four key cultural characteristics that are prerequisites for creating a high-performance culture, characteristics that are interrelated and mutually reinforcing: self-initiation, trust, interdependence, and partnering.

Self-Initiation

On one level self-initiation is simply employees taking responsibility for, and ownership of, their own performance and learning. However, as much as any of the ideas presented in this book, self-initiation represents a significant shift from industrial-era to knowledge-era paradigms. It has far-reaching implications for both individuals and organizations and how they relate.

In the industrial era the employment contract between employer and employee was based simply on the idea that the employer provided the employee with work, often for a lifetime, and in exchange the employee offered the organization loyalty. It was a passive state, in which the employee essentially said: "If I don't rock the apple cart, if I do what I'm told, I will in exchange be eligible for a promised future with the organization. The organization will look after me."

Given that established corporations rarely went out of business, and with equal infrequency downsized, such a loyalty contract could work—albeit with clear role delineations, and tensions, between managerial and general employee groups.

However, just as the rules of business have changed for organizations, so have rules for individuals. In the knowledge era loyalty-based contracts are becoming increasingly obsolete. No organization can, with any real level of integrity, offer employees a job for life due to ever-changing job requirements, organizational structures, mergers and acquisitions, and corporate failures. As a consequence there is an emerging requirement to forge a new knowledge-era template for organization-employee relationships. Given that it's our employees who must implement our strategies, reengaging the employee base is a central challenge for managers in mitigating the risk of strategic failure.

The new organization-employee relationship that we've been experimenting with is one based not on the entitlement contracts of the industrial era, but rather on commitments from both parties. In this relationship the individual says, "I will commit to create value in the corporation in exchange for the ability to create new capabilities for myself that enhance my market worth." The organization commits to providing the environment in which the individual can create such capabilities. The conductive organization also ensures that robust knowledge capturing and sharing processes are in place to transform individual capabilities into organizational capabilities.

It's incumbent on organizations to view employees (and for individuals to view themselves) first and foremost as *businesses of one*, who are offering something of value (their capabilities that meet the performance expectations of the organization) in exchange for something that they value.

However, this new commitment contract can only be realized when individuals subscribe to it from a position of self-initiation. Self-initiation means they take responsibility for their own performance and learning. Employees must occupy a mental space where they aren't waiting for instructions or the next training program to be offered, but take the initiative to find the knowledge or develop the capabilities that they need.

Although we believe that a contract based on loyalty is now obsolete, we're certainly not saying that we should be looking to recruit employees for short periods only. Given the raging war for talent within most sectors, a contract based on commitment can actually be a strong differentiator in the competitive marketplace for high-quality employees. Talented employees are always looking to further develop their stock of individual capabilities and will be drawn to organizations that offer this opportunity. These employees typically arrive at the organization already with a self-initiated mindset.

Interestingly, moving employees toward self-initiation calls into question the validity of conventional measures of employee loyalty or the satisfaction indicators that we once believed led to loyalty. Like the assessment of customer loyalty and satisfaction, these measures are of little real value today. Employees can be loyal (i.e., stay with the organization for a prolonged period) or satisfied without being committed to the organization. They may, even if contentedly, just be going through the motions.

Overcoming an entitlement-based mindset is not without significant challenges. We've observed that becoming self-initiated can be a struggle for many people who find an entitlement-based culture much more comfortable. The concept of a self-initiated employee is also difficult for many managers who prefer a more traditional, conservative mode of providing leadership. Most individuals will require coaching and support in making the transition to self-initiation, to become aware that there is a powerful connector between self-initiation and their own career and financial security.

Trust

The second critical cultural characteristic for creating a highly conductive organization is trust. A central proposition of this book is that trust should permeate all relationships that the organization enters into—with customers, partners, and employees.

Trust is essential for building the level of collaboration required for unimpeded knowledge flow. People will naturally hold back from contributing to relationships that they feel to be untrustworthy. Just as customers will not commit to suppliers they don't trust, employees won't fully commit to organizations or to colleagues if they feel trust is absent. Mistrust is one of the biggest barriers to conductivity.

Trust has many components. In a trust-based environment employees are willing to contribute their knowledge to the organization or team because they know that their contribution will be recognized and that they will have equal access to other people's knowledge. Where there is trust, employees are confident that they are being supported in achieving their goals, in being the best they can be, and that they are supporting worthwhile organizational goals.

Employees must trust that they can contribute their ideas, opinions, hopes, and aspirations without fear of ridicule. They also must trust that they won't be penalized for failures, but will be able to use failures as opportunities for learning. The most meaningful way to enhance the trust level in an organization is to practice leadership in line with clearly identified corporate values. Courageous leadership that stands for clearly identified values will serve as the foundation for a healthy dialogue across the organization. This leads to mutual accountability where everyone is responsible for behaving in line with the defined values of the organization. Leaders create opportunities for productive conversations to take place around issues or problems as they emerge, which constantly renews the contextual understanding employees have of choices being made by the organization.

Interdependence and Partnerships

Employees recognize that more value is created for the customer, for themselves personally, and for their partners when they agree to work collaboratively—where there is interdependence. People make themselves successful by helping to make others successful. Interdependence is a natural environment for generalized reciprocity.

A culture of interdependence is one in which employees listen to each other with the goal of creating new capabilities. It's the opposite of a culture of counterdependence, in which employees compete with each other and actively deny the value that others bring to the conversation (see Figure 7.4). Interdependence is important across all relationships in the networked value chain—with suppliers, partners, and distributors as well as between functions, teams, and employees. With conductivity defined as *the capability to effectively transmit quality knowledge throughout the organization as well as with and between customers and employees*, it can only work at any reasonable level where a culture of interdependence exists.

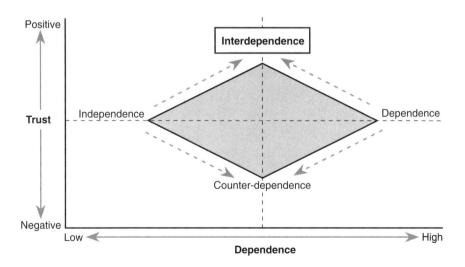

Figure 7.4 Interdependence

Self-initiation, trust, and interdependence allow the individual to partner without reserve. But partnership can only take place between two people who aren't interacting in a dependent mode. As self-initiated individuals, they must stand whole and have a foundation for discovering how they complement one another—only then can they move forward in a partnership with confidence. Any other partnership (i.e., where one or both are dependent) has a high likelihood of eventual failure because the partners will reach a point of distrust that will irrevocably damage the partnership.

Partnerships may be short-term or long-term, team-based or more loosely individually based; they may be project-specific or built around communities of practice. What's important is that a common purpose is identified and that all participants are committed to a common goal.

As an example of short-term partnerships, Armstrong brings together cross-functional teams for 60-day projects aimed at strategic initiatives. Well-defined expectations are set at the start of the projects, and the individual team employees are responsible for delivering the goals in the allotted time frame. The team is then disbanded, and new teams are configured to address other strategic requirements. Such rapid team configuration, disbanding, and reconfiguration requires strong partnership skills, trust, and self-initiation. Also crucial is a shared sense of core values.

Partnership also necessitates a sense of collective ownership, where employees take joint responsibility for cocreating the organization's future and recognize that by doing so they are shaping their own futures.

Possessing the right culture can also prove very attractive to partners outside the organization. In the financial services industry, it can be a challenge to attract agents to the organization. However, at Clarica this wasn't much of a problem simply because agents were attracted by the belief that Clarica wanted a partnering relationship with its agents, would support the agents in developing their own capabilities, and was an organization that placed significant importance in maintaining high levels of trust.

Assessing Culture

Culture, as with any other capability, has to evolve in line with changing marketplace circumstances and should be actively managed to ensure that it doesn't atrophy or become a barrier to performance. With culture and values being so intertwined, an executive team at Clarica put together what was called the Value of Your Voice. These quarterly sessions proved a useful tool for assessing the evolution of employee values and attitudes toward the existing culture. Similar sessions have also been implemented within Armstrong.

The findings from the Value of Your Voice workshops were reported to the executive committee, who initiated interventions to address areas of concern. Corrective actions were then communicated to employees, and the outcomes of these interventions could be monitored in future workshops.

Conclusion

As a key organizational capability in a highly conductive organization, culture is the gatekeeper that regulates behavior. It's the trump card that either wins the trick or loses the hand. Understanding employee, customer, and partner values and finding the commonly held values with the organization is a first step in identifying the willingness of people to work toward common goals with expected behaviors. By shaping individual mindsets in a constructive manner, organizations have the ability to move a culture to be supportive of its strategies as long as the historical context is valued.

Self-initiation, trust, interdependence, and partnerships are the four prominent cultural characteristics of a highly conductive organization. With executive sponsorship, employee endorsement, and customer enthusiasm, the journey to discover core values and align culture to strategic needs is a capability-generating exercise that continually renews commitment and deepens relationships.

Emerging Principles

■ Having a culture that is engaged in fulfilling the customer imperative relies on having employee values focused in the same direction—on the customer.

■ Employees are more likely to commit to an organization whose
values are congruent to their own.

■ Values are internalized ideals. They are priorities that guide us in
making everyday choices and shape our behaviour.

■ We need diversity to respond to the diverse values of the customer.

■ Adherence to well-defined corporate values allows the organization
to accelerate change without losing the trust of its employees.

■ Culture is a key enabler of business performance. It can make or
break strategies.

■ Organizational cultures have very deep roots that have spread out
unseen yet are pervasive through time.

■ Attempting to change culture without acknowledging with great
respect and humility its historical roots is disastrous.

■ Four key cultural characteristics are prerequisites for creating a high
performance culture: self-initiation, trust, interdependence, and
partnering.

■ Self-initiation represents a major shift from industrial to knowledge
paradigms.

■ In the knowledge era, loyalty-based contracts are becoming increasingly obsolete.

■ Reengaging the employee base is a central challenge for the managers in mitigating risk of strategic failure.

- It's incumbent on organizations to view employees first and foremost as a business of one.

- Trust should permeate all relationships that the organization enters into—with customers, employees, and partners.

- Mistrust is one of the biggest barriers to conductivity.

- A culture of interdependence is one in which employees listen to each other with the goal of creating new capabilities.

- Culture is the gatekeeper that regulates behavior.

References

1. Hall, B.D. (1995). *Values Shift: A Guide to Personal and Organizational Transformation.* Rockport, MA: Twin Lights Publishing.
2. Schein, E. (2001). *Organizational Culture and Leadership.* San Francisco: Jossey-Bass Publishers.
3. Creelman, J. (1999). *Driving Corporate Culture for Business Success.* London: Business Intelligence.

8

Structure: The Custodians of Conductivity

Introduction

The third key organizational capability in a highly conductive organization is structure—the arrangement or grouping of people and responsibilities into particular roles as well as the relationships between and the integration of these various groups to form the whole (see Figure 8.1). To enable an unimpeded flow of high-quality knowledge at an accelerated pace, we need to rethink traditional organizational structures and create new approaches that are aligned to our strategy and to our capability to calibrate to customer needs.

Customer calibration requires new capabilities that are applied externally as well as practiced internally. If high-trust relationships, partnering mindsets, and meaningful conversations are all qualities that we expect to exhibit with our customers and value-creation network partners, then we must have structures that are aligned to support the internal practice of these dimensions.

To fully discuss all of the structural changes necessary to achieve breakthrough performance in the knowledge era would take volumes. In this chapter we start the conversation about the need to restructure, we outline the basic components of functional configurations that support a highly conductive organization, and illustrate how Clarica and Armstrong reorganized areas responsible for championing their evolution to more highly conductive organizations.

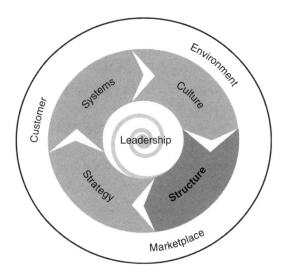

Figure 8.1   Structure—A Core Organizational Capability

Functional Configurations

In Chapter 1 we saw that industrial-era organizations were configured to fit a make-and-sell production model. They were precisely defined, with separate roles delineated for functions such as purchasing, manufacturing, sales, marketing, and finance. Each function had its own vertical reporting structure and more often than not a discrete culture. Each function was further broken down into narrower departments. Horizontal cross-functional relationships were typically poorly defined and strained, often to the point of creating an internal culture of blame and self-protection.

As newer functions such as human resources (HR) and, more recently, information technology (IT) emerged to support organizational activities, they too were constructed according to the functional designs of the industrial era, with the same limitations and internal foci. They became new silos functioning in semi-isolation from the traditional silos.

Impeding Knowledge Flows

From the perspective of the conductive organization, it's easy to see how the existence of so many functional silos creates barriers to unimpeded knowledge flows. We're not questioning the integrity or value of employees who work in conventional functions. They have typically expended significant personal effort to become experts in their domains and provide value to their organizations. Instead, we're suggesting that in today's environment it's necessary to more effectively deploy, or reassemble, the talents of these highly professional people to create a high-performance organization.

Conventional functional units that are each allocated sole ownership of large parts of the value chain impede the flow of knowledge. When marketing or customer service has sole responsibility for the customer, and human resources has sole responsibility for the employee-base, we have barriers to interfacing our human capital and customer capital.

To deepen relationships at the customer and employee interface, we need to create ways to organize employees to ensure that the quality of the customer relationship and the employees' ownership of that relationship continue to grow. It's difficult to seamlessly facilitate this convergence if one department "owns" the customers and another department the employees. These separate organizational pockets, with different mandates, preoccupations, and vocabularies, cause the organization to lose the level of coherence required to optimize human capital and customer capital.

The same problem exists with HR and IT. A significant part of the IT mandate today is to raise our information technology to the high levels required to obtain a knowledge yield from transactions. This knowledge yield depends to a large extent on whether the technology infrastructure is shaped to enhance the performance of people and the organization as a whole. This yield cannot be achieved without people management processes designed to attain the levels of interdependence and collaboration required for people to exchange knowledge. People management plays a key role in leveraging the technology infrastructure to its full potential. As we move toward more conductive organizations, separating IT and HR mandates will become more and more problematic for organizations.

In the industrial era, when the value created by intangible assets was less important, this lack of coherence wasn't as costly. As participants in the knowledge era, with our key competitive advantage coming from intangible assets, we can no longer afford the organizational disconnects that presently exist.

Cross-Functional Collaboration

Over recent years we've witnessed moves by most organizations to break down the barriers between functions. Putting in place processes and structures that encourage cross-functional collaboration has become accepted practice. We've also seen the emergence of organizational leaders with job titles that describe management of core organizational processes that cut through functional departments—a vice president for strategic capabilities as one example. This trend reflects a growing recognition that process management is potentially more customer-focused and efficient than a purely functional approach.

We've also been subjected to a barrage of books, conferences, and consultancy offerings focused on topics such as "creating a value-adding HR (or IT or finance) function." These programs have as a core proposition that, for the knowledge era, the survival of functions and the career progression of functional professionals require the adoption of an organization-wide, rather than function-specific, performance perspective.

Although these attempts to break out of functional confines are positive, there is still a danger that cross-functional configurations that continue to leave the functions intact typically suffer the territorial turf wars, self-protection, and political games that have always been a feature of department-to-department relationships.

The most exciting organizational structural experiments over the next decade will be dismantling industrial-era functions and replacing them with knowledge-era configurations. No function will be left untouched, and it is conceivable that no conventional function will be left standing in a formation that we recognize today.

Limitations of Traditional Human Resources Configuration

For the knowledge era, the conventional human resources function is essentially obsolete. One of its principal shortcomings is that the function was originally created as a filter between the organization and the individual to address distrust between the two. An outcome of this intermediary role was that HR was largely treated with suspicion by both sides. Management saw HR as the champions of the employee, while the employee believed HR to be the mouthpiece of management. Management often failed to consider HR a strategic partner because they saw HR as speaking for the individual in isolation from what was required to meet customer needs.

The deployment of any regular intermediary between an employee who holds managerial responsibilities and other employees typically acts as a barrier to knowledge flow, and certainly diminishes the trust relationship. Moreover, intermediation is contrary to our belief in the importance of self-initiation. Self-initiated individuals need to link directly with their managers without an intermediary.

Finally, the forces of the market have radically altered the employment contract between the organization and the individual. Yet HR still largely functions according to industrial-era entitlement approaches, often criticized by management as being too slow to adapt to the dynamics of the knowledge economy. As a result, the HR function is further sidelined.

The Strategic Capabilities Unit

New configurations were introduced at Clarica in the late 1990s and more recently at Armstrong. Both organizations had been consider-

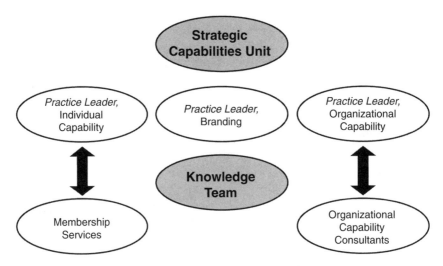

Figure 8.2   Clarica's Strategic Capabilities Unit

ing the challenge of how to create an internal dynamic that could best leverage their human, structural, and customer capital in a holistic manner. The result was an organizational focus on strategic capabilities.

At Clarica, a Strategic Capabilities Unit was formed (see Figure 8.2), aligned with the Knowledge Capital Model (see Figure 3.2). Individual capability and membership services groups work to increase human capital. The organizational capability practice works to increase structural capital, and the brand team works to increase customer capital. A shared purpose of increasing the flow of knowledge throughout the organization provides the focal point for and integration of the groups.

The Strategic Capabilities Unit is configured to provide a central direction for the capability, relationship, cultural, knowledge sharing, and learning performance dimensions. While the unit doesn't own any one of these dimensions, it champions and stewards the development of central practices that are networked throughout the functional areas of the organization. It's critical that ownership of these dimensions is avoided. If ownership takes hold, we'll quickly see the re-emergence of the silos, with all the performance inhibitions that we're endeavoring to replace.

Ready, Willing, and Able

Considered against conventional functional structures, the unit integrates what was the HR function and encompasses required expertise from marketing and IT. This new unit is charged with helping to ensure that the organization is ready, willing, and able to deliver to business goals (see Table 8.1).

Executive Status

For the unit to be legitimized and capable of delivering to its mandate, the head of the unit held executive management status. This position signalled that creating the unit was seen as a strategic imperative by Clarica's CEO and senior executive team. It also

Table 8.1 Goals in Creating a Ready, Willing, and Able Organization

Individual Capability (Ready)	Organizational Capability (Willing)	Knowledge Architecture (Able)
Deliver, shape, and model *people management processes, practices, and tools* to meet the business needs of the organization.	*Align* leadership, culture, processes, structure, and strategy.	■ Fully integrate *knowledge architecture*, linking repositories of knowledge, communities of practice, and members of the organization.
	■ Facilitate *change management* process.	■ Business practices fully leverage the *knowledge tools*, resulting in increased effectiveness, agility, and innovation.
	■ Enable *knowledge* capture and sharing.	■ Accelerate development of individual capability through self-initiated *learning* opportunities.

ensured that any political grievances (such as might have arisen around the perceived weakening of functional power) could be overcome. The goal was always to involve everyone in this transformational journey. The parallel efforts to shape a values-based culture across the organization reinforced the new direction for the unit. Everyone could see that bold attempts to shape a new culture required equally bold approaches to reconfigure the structure in order to safeguard and leverage the new culture.

Individual Capability Practice

The purpose of the Individual Capability Practice was to ensure that people management processes were conducive to high levels of performance for individuals and the organization as a whole. A key focus of this practice was to shape people management policies and practices that enabled self-initiation and collective ownership. Employees were encouraged to own their performance and development and not be dependent on their managers or a separate body, such as HR. The Individual Capability Practice developed approaches for performance self-assessment, 90-Day Plans, and values assessment.

Membership Services

To increase employee capabilities to better meet customer expectations, Clarica integrated all HR functions into the Strategic Capabilities Unit, refocused them, and renamed the new subunit Membership Services. The name Membership Services was chosen to reflect the belief that the term "human resources" objectifies people and suggests a commodity the organization owns and can do with as it likes—a notion that conflicts with the knowledge-era precept of generalized reciprocity. Clarica's executives recognized that to live its core values, people needed to share a strong sense of membership in the organization and not to feel like an anonymous resource or cog in the wheel.

Membership Services was organized to provide a four-tiered service approach to meet employee needs (see Figure 8.3). Tier 0, the first level of service, was designed to be self-service. All people-management policies and processes were fully outlined on the corporate intranet and accessible by all employees from their desktops. To achieve their objective of having 70% of all member-related transactions serviced at Tier 0, Clarica considered all new policies and processes in light of how they would be provided at Tier 0.

Tier 0 offerings ranged from enabling employees to correct their personal details in the organization's files, to hiring a new employee, to accessing calculators that helped employees identify their pension value.

Membership Service's home page was the main vehicle for Tier 0 delivery. It included general information about the group, details of people policies and practices, a section called "manager's how-to" and another called "member's how-to," and functional information on specific topics such as benefits, compensation, payroll, policies, and recruiting.

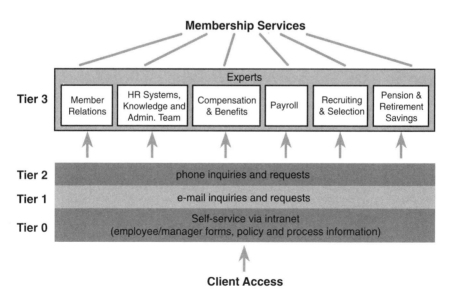

Figure 8.3 Clarica's Membership Services' Tiered Approach

The manager's how-to section provided managers with the requisite knowledge to process bonuses, complete transfers, and fill a vacancy. By clicking on the "filling a vacancy" link, the inquiring manager would be given a detailed step-by-step template for the hiring process, including creating a job posting, assessing candidates, and understanding staffing and transition policies.

For questions that required further elaboration, managers and other employees could move to Tier 1, where they could email a Membership Services Representative. It was then the responsibility of the representative to find the answer and respond quickly. If the employee preferred, or if the question required a contextual explanation, Tier 2 was available for telephone follow-up by a representative.

At Tier 3, employees could access Individual Capability Consultants, who provided personal interventions to resolve more complex issues, perhaps helping a manager think through and articulate a staffing strategy or facilitate a coaching relationship between an experienced employee and a recent recruit. Tier 3 was also the level at which Clarica dealt with sensitive issues such as a case of conflict between employees or sexual harassment.

Individual Capability Architects

Within the Individual Capability Practice, five architects were responsible for developing policies and processes required for different areas, including career development, capability mapping, recruitment, and compensation, incentives, and benefits.

Working with a firm called Recruit Soft, Clarica created a web-enabled resourcing approach by which the Individual Capability Practice could craft innovative processes. Employees could manage their career development via the intranet. All open project assignments were placed on a website, with the required assignment profile. Not only could employees apply for projects when assignments arose, but they could submit their resume to the site and be instantly alerted when a match was made between an open or new assignment and their skills. This resourcing tool was not just for internal use but was made available to external people interested in working for Clarica. Potential recruits submitted their profile to the site and were contacted immediately when a match was made.

A sixth architect within the Individual Capability Practice, responsible for learning, became part of the Knowledge Team, helping to ensure that knowledge and learning became fully integrated.

Organizational Capability Practice

The Organizational Capability Practice had the mandate to ensure the alignment of leadership, culture, structure, and strategy—the core organizational capabilities. The team included a leader and 12 organizational capability consultants. The consultants were located in the business units, integrating Strategic Capabilities with their internal business partners.

Most large projects or any significant business team within Clarica had an organizational capability consultant working as a full-fledged team member. One of the Organizational Capability Practice's contributions was to facilitate and accelerate the changes these business teams aimed to achieve. The consultants operated as a community of practice, with the Organizational Capability Practice leader acting as the facilitator. They had a responsibility as a community to enhance the change readiness of the organization as a whole, to build explicit knowledge for this purpose, and to share their tacit knowledge.

As they oversaw and facilitated the adoption of effective change management processes, the consultants played a key role in support of organizational transformation and renewal. Their work served to ensure that all employees were engaged in representing the brand and the value proposition of the organization to its customers. They supported the managers of their business units in placing their strategic initiatives into a cohesive organizational framework that could be readily understood.

An important part of the Organizational Capability Practice mandate was its contribution to the evolution of a culture that gives full expression to the core values of the organization. They mentored individuals in aligning their leadership practices to the core values of the organization. At the team level, they maintained a clear vision of how they would achieve team goals through the application of core values.

The Brand Practice

In the Strategic Capabilities Unit model, the Brand Practice sits between the Individual and Organizational Capability Practices. This placement is purposeful as it provides a customer dimension to the focus of the unit. Central to Strategic Capabilities's mandate was to increase the capabilities needed at all levels to build deep relationships with the customer. The brand promise applies equally to employees as well as customers, so the Brand Practice helps ensure congruence of internal and external brand. Furthermore, being placed with a Strategic Capabilities Unit ensures that the brand promise is formally recognized as a strategic capability of the corporation and not just a clever piece of marketing.

Objectives for the Brand Practice included:

- Accelerate development of Clarica's distinctive market presence and its impact on the growth of the business.
- Focus on the customer experience provided by its agents with the support of the services and solutions Clarica had to offer.
- Develop specific action plans to accelerate the building of brand capabilities throughout the entire corporation.
- Define, communicate, and leverage the linkage between employee and customer branding.
- Foster the adoption of "clarity through dialogue" as part of how the organization conducted everyday business.

Clarica CEO and president Robert M. Astley said at the corporation's Annual General meeting in 2001, "The brand promise *clarity through dialogue* is at the core of our business model at Clarica. We have built our business on the strength of relationships to deliver on our brand promise." (1) The executive management team believed that the brand should be managed as a strategic capability, with a natural alignment to the Strategic Capabilities Unit.

Knowledge Team

The Knowledge Team embodied the sociotechnical approach that was at the heart of Clarica's overall capability and relationship-building efforts. Its role was to provide the technology, tools, and processes necessary for all employees to acquire the knowledge they needed to acquire in real time, to best support colleagues, and to effectively serve the customer.

The Knowledge Team was responsible for both the "knowledge as stock" and "knowledge as practice" aspects of the knowledge strategy. The Knowledge Depot was created on the corporate intranet to access the collective information of the organization. And communities of practice were sponsored to support knowledge exchange. The Knowledge Team shaped the technology platform and the collaborative processes that defined the architecture providing access to knowledge repositories and membership in communities of practice. It was also responsible for the ongoing development of Clarica Connects, the corporate intranet. As part of its role, the Team established a collaborative approach, working with knowledge stewards across the business units to design features and maintain content.

In addition to developing an integrated architecture at the organizational level, the Knowledge Team supported specific knowledge initiatives in the business units. These projects demonstrated the potential business impact of knowledge tools and processes across the organization, developing cross-functional approaches that leveraged synergies and enabled knowledge flow.

New Organizing Structures at Armstrong

The evolution of organizing structures at Armstrong demonstrates the transformation process underway to become a more highly conductive organization. In the early 1990s, Armstrong was serving markets in Canada, the United States, the United Kingdom, Europe, and the Middle East with a full line of products in relative autonomy from the parent organization. Each group had traditional functional departments reporting to general managers or managing directors. There was little cross-functional interaction, and within the functional areas there were few standardized processes. As globalization forces emerged and free trade was implemented in North America, the need for improved customer service became a priority.

The first phase of transformation was initiated by two strategies: developing a global product focus and developing a common IT business process. Armstrong de-emphasized local autonomy and legal entities and implemented common IT systems and processes across the organization. However, each operating unit was designated as a global center of product excellence. The global product teams provided expertise to local sales efforts in a matrix system.

Each product team had global profit and loss, manufacturing, research and development, and marketing responsibilities. Business units were smaller and driven through a complex matrix to compete by product type at the global marketplace level. Traditional legal entity boundaries dissolved, and the traditional functional silos within product groups were transformed into tightly knit teams. The IT structures and processes became an entrepreneurial framework in which these business units could easily and effectively tap into the company's larger network system.

By the mid 1990s, Armstrong was well on its way to developing a more self-initiated culture based on the values of learning and collaborating. It had also gained a deeper understanding of the business's significant intangible assets. Through the application of the Enterprise Capital Model, Armstrong began to explore the customer-based needs of its markets. As a first step, it globalized its marketing function in an effort to more deeply understand the value-added products and services required by its customers. Armstrong also found from the analysis of value network mapping that customer clusters were forming and calibrated approaches to bring customers with like needs together (see Figure 4.4).

With the Customer Dialer (see Chapter 4) putting the customer at the center of the organization and calibrating capabilities to meet customer needs, the organization has now evolved to focus on customer clusters. Strategies are aligned with organizational and individual capabilities and core values held by the organization and the customers to add value at both the customer and the customer cluster levels. Each customer cluster shares value propositions with other parts of the organization, and Armstrong has become more aware of the intangible flows of value and knowledge created by a deeper understanding of customer needs.

To facilitate these structural changes, Armstrong created a Management Board, consisting of managing shareholders and advisors, and a Leadership Board, representing the local geographic regions and functional capabilities of the organization. The Leadership Board is responsible for contributing to the strategic development process and the implementation of the strategic and business plans. This team is collectively responsible for delivering the performance of the business (see team leadership model Figure 10.4).

Armstrong's evolution from a traditional functional structure to global product business units to customer cluster focus has taken the organization through a huge learning process that has been enabled by significant IT support structures. A new and vital culture focused on innovating with the customer has emerged.

Conclusion

Both Clarica and Armstrong have found that new organizational structures better support their evolution to a more highly conductive organization. Specifically, both organizations have found that we can:

- Leverage branding to develop a distinctive customer and employee experience
- Facilitate the accelerated development of individual and organizational capabilities

- Support the effective generation and transfer of knowledge across the organization
- Support accelerated change to realize business strategies
- Reinforce self-initiation of employees
- Support a high-performance organizational climate
- Remove "organizational walls" through communities of practice.

Customer-calibrated structures help shift the organization from a make-and-sell to a sense-and-respond configuration, establish new mindsets, and create first-mover advantage in its marketplaces. With the strategic capabilities units in particular, we've taken early steps in rethinking internal configurations for the knowledge era.

The continuous evolution, or rethinking and recalibrating, of how work is organized and accomplished is a key competency for the knowledge era. A perpetual question for all knowledge-era organizations will be whether they're arranged appropriately for the rapid creation of capabilities and the deepening of all their relationships. Asking this question at every step of their evolution may guarantee that emerging configurations for the knowledge era don't repeat the turf wars and performance-depleting behaviors of their industrial-era ancestors.

Emerging Principles

- The most exciting organizational structural experiments over the next decade will be dismantling industrial-era functions and replacing them with knowledge-era configurations.

- The conventional human resources function is essentially obsolete.

- Employees need to be self-initiated in their own development plans.

- If the organization is to live its core values, people need to share a strong sense of membership in the organization.

Reference

1. Robert M. Astley, President and Chief Executive Officer, Clarica Life Insurance Company. Keynote address to the 2001 Annual and Special Meeting, Toronto, Canada, April 2002.

9

Systems: Generating Capabilities

Introduction

The fourth core organizational capability in the conductive organization is systems—the assembly of all horizontal and vertical processes across the organization that enable it to implement its strategy (see Figure 9.1). We use the term *system* to mean a connected arrangement of elements that make a whole. Its use is compared with physical systems like the solar system or an ecosystem, or in the context of the human body, the circulatory system or nervous system. The use of systems in an organizational context is not limited to a focus on computer systems.

An organization is a complex system of many different processes—processes to track finances, develop new products, deliver customer service, and create the technology infrastructure. All of these systems work in concert to accomplish the organization's strategy, meet stakeholder expectations, and deliver products and services to customers.

As with structures, changes to systems to support breakthrough performance are many, but in all instances, they are customer calibrated. One of the key system groups linked to the customer are the systems used to generate capabilities. Capabilities are the link between strategy and performance—the fulcrum on which breakthrough performance relies. The ability to generate capabilities in real time to meet the changing needs of the customer is integral to achieving breakthrough performance.

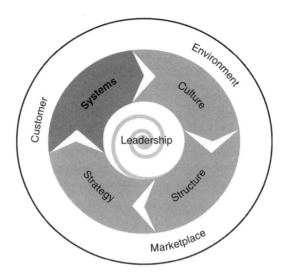

Figure 9.1   Systems—A Core Organizational Capability

Knowledge Architecture

Within the knowledge strategy is a blueprint that outlines the system structure for generating capabilities referred to as *knowledge architecture*. While the organization strategy with its embedded knowledge strategy provides the vision and direction for transforming the organization to a higher state of conductivity, the knowledge architecture outlines the key process components that facilitate the actions needed to reach the strategy's goals.

The knowledge architecture used to enable capability generation consists of two key processes: knowledge access and knowledge exchange (see Figure 9.2).

Knowledge access creates a platform for managing explicit knowledge. It provides a way to build and use an organization's stocks. Over 30 knowledge managers at Clarica ensure that knowledge databases directly support the information needs of all employees. In addition, considerable attention is given to how knowledge databases are linked into a navigable network, guaranteeing that explicit knowledge is easily accessed and made available to employees at

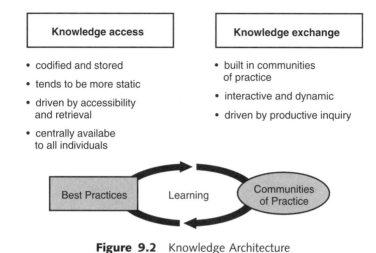

Figure 9.2   Knowledge Architecture

their desktops. Knowledge access also includes all the preparatory work of database design, codification, storage, and display.

Knowledge exchange provides opportunities to share tacit knowledge by implementing ways to connect people to people, facilitate communities, and identify expertise networks. It channels the flow of knowledge between individuals. Teams working on projects usually encounter an issue that they haven't seen before. They need information on how to resolve it. They may need more than stored, explicit knowledge. They need advice about assessing the situation and finding a solution from someone who has had a similar experience. They need the combined resources of explicit and tacit knowledge in order to gain a level of understanding that will give them the confidence to take effective action.

Knowledge and Learning

Learning is the primary approach for generating capabilities. In a conductive organization, the knowledge architecture supports these processes, which can be viewed, in themselves, as complex systems that create knowledge. To recap, we define knowledge as *the capa-*

bility to take effective action and learning as *the process of turning information into knowledge to take effective action.* These definitions illustrate the strong relationship between knowledge and learning. Learning is the process of making meaning—of internalizing information, whereas knowledge forms the basis for how solutions are applied. Before knowledge can flow, it's important to ensure that the learning process has filtered and validated information as value-creating knowledge stocks.

The exchange of tacit knowledge happens in many ways within organizations through countless formal and informal mechanisms (e.g., email, meetings, discussions around the water cooler). A significant amount of this knowledge eventually leaks out of the organization because little effort is expended in facilitating its exchange and in its conversion into a strategic capability. However, the systematic management of knowledge exchange needs to become a strategic capability as organizations struggle to find new ways to make sense of the massive amount of information available.

Cultural Underpinnings

The first condition for knowledge exchange is that the cultural characteristics of self-initiation, trust, interdependence, and partnership are in place. Effective knowledge exchange requires high-trust relationships and relies on employees' coalescing around a set of core values on which they agree and to which they commit. Where high-trust, values-based relationships are formed, employees are more likely to proactively share knowledge among themselves and with their customers.

Self-initiation is a fundamental condition for a rich knowledge exchange. With the vast amounts of knowledge being amassed by individuals, it's impossible for organizations to effectively manage knowledge flows without the voluntary involvement of employees. Employees must assume responsibility for knowledge exchange as a key part of their learning and capability development—of the way they do their work. They must see the benefits of knowledge exchange to themselves, the members of their team, and their customers. In terms of capability generation, generalized reciprocity is a catalyst for sharing as opposed to hoarding knowledge.

Communities of Practice

One way to promote knowledge exchange is through communities of practice. These groups of people joined by a common goal of improving a particular practice have gained renewed purpose enabled by new technology. Clarica had a wide range of formal and informal communities of practice that facilitated tacit knowledge exchange and contributed to building explicit knowledge stocks in specialized areas. As part of its knowledge strategy, Clarica invested considerable resources in providing processes and systems to support the development and growth of communities.

We define communities of practice in a strategic context as: *groups of self-governing people whose practice is aligned with strategic imperatives and who are challenged to create shareholder value by generating knowledge and increasing capabilities.* We shaped this definition to illustrate self-initiation (self-governing) and clearly describe the strategic nature of such communities. The core proposition of communities has to reflect the organization's strategies. In other words, the issues and problems addressed by these communities must be relevant to the strategic challenges of the organization. Communities exist to provide value to the organization and their members, and not to become insular, exclusive clubs.

Different Types of Communities

Communities of practice come in various shapes and sizes. At Clarica, communities ranged from 20 to 150 employees. Some communities were informal, loose networks of people who only occasionally sought each other's advice, while others were highly structured groups who collaborated as an integral part of their working day. To illustrate the differences between types of communities of practice, Saint-Onge and Wallace (1) identified characteristics of three forms of communities of practice—informal, supported, and structured (see Table 9.1). All three types should exist and be nurtured for knowledge exchange to effectively generate capabilities.

Communities Are Built on Trust

Trust underpins all internal and external relationships and is fundamental for successful communities of practice. Community members must be willing to ask questions that will draw on the experience, the knowledge, and the insights of their colleagues. However, members will be unwilling to place questions within a community of practice if there is a low level of trust. A safe environment must exist if members are to honestly admit that they don't know something. In order for creative problem solving to work, community members must be ready to engage in a conversation robust enough to test one another's assumptions. People must be willing to explore issues, build on one another's ideas in a constructive manner, and change each other's viewpoints. These objectives can only be achieved in a trusting environment.

Members must also trust that their contribution will make a difference and will be recognized. Communities of practice are extremely difficult to create if the trust reservoir of the organization has been depleted—if individuals feel that their participation is not recognized or their contributions are used inappropriately.

Table 9.1 Types of Communities of Practice

	Informal	Supported	Structured
Purpose	Provide a discussion forum for people with affinity of interests	Build capability for a given business or competency area	Provide a cross-functional platform for members who have common objectives
Sponsorship	No organizational sponsor	One or more managers	Business team/senior management
Mandate	Jointly defined by members	Jointly defined by members and sponsor(s)	Defined by sponsor(s) with endorsement of members
Evolution	Organic development	Purposeful development, co-determined by sponsor(s) and members	Organizationally determined development based on business objectives
Main Outcomes	—Individual capability development —Codification of knowledge useful to members —Higher levels of trust and collaboration in the organization —Greater retention of talent	—Sharing and building of organizational knowledge —Focused development of capability relevant to achieving organizational goals —Greater collaboration across organizational segments	—Systematic orchestration of communities of practice —Speed of execution —Enterprise-wide alignment —Creative solutions —Enhanced effectiveness of organizational structure

Table 9.1 Types of Communities of Practice (*continued*)

	Informal	Supported	Structured
Accountability	Not attached to formal accountability structure	Contributes to the realization of business objectives	Forms an inherent part of the accountability structure with specific objectives to achieve
Organizational Support	—General endorsement of communities of practice —Provision of standard collaboration tools	—Discretionary managerial support in terms of resources and participation —Supplemented array of tools and facilitation support	—Full-fledged organizational support on the same basis as organizational segments —Budget allocation as part of the business plan
Infrastructure	—Meets face-to-face for primary contact —Has a means of communication for secondary contact	—Uses collaborative tools —Meets face-to-face on a regular basis	—Uses sophisticated technology infrastructure to support collaboration and store knowledge objects generated in the community —Highly enabled by technology
Visibility	So natural, may not even be noticed	Visible to colleagues affected by the community's contribution to practice	Highly visible to the organization through targeted communication efforts that are stewarded by sponsors.

Community of Practice Benefits

When communities of practice are effective vehicles for knowledge exchange, they contribute to the organization, the community itself, its members, and the customers they serve. Specifically effective communities can:

- **Help resolve issues quickly with creative outcomes.** Members of a community of practice get to know and trust one another's expertise. They understand the generalized reciprocity—if they answer a query quickly, their own query will be similarly treated. The frame of reference that they gradually build together allows them to put forward questions that are readily understood by other members. This level of mutual understanding also helps ensure that the advice provided is relevant and to the point and brings the collective experience to the table to create solutions.
- **Transmitting learning and sharing knowledge.** Mistakes are often repeated in organizations at substantial costs. Communities serve to test ideas and discover whether they have been tried in the past. Communities become an ideal forum for exchanging ideas and best practices across the organization. Multigenerational membership allows more experienced members to share their knowledge in an unobtrusive, natural manner. The participation of members with different lengths of experience ensures that the knowledge exchanged stays up to date and valid.
- **Accelerating capability generation through collaboration and learning.** Learning is most effective when it comes from peers and applies to concrete work situations. Communities of practice provide a natural channel for learning. Questions are answered on the basis of experience and validated by others who have faced similar real-life situations. Consequently, communities of practice are intimately tied to action in the work-

place and therefore congruent with the learning is work and work is learning principle.

- **Attracting and retaining talent.** A strong sense of belonging to a community within the workplace is a key contributor to retention. In the anonymous world of large and complex multisite organizations, communities of practice provide a sense of connection between people. They make people feel that they belong in a social context that is conducive to their development and the fulfillment of their potential.

- **Serving as a platform for external networks.** As communities of practice are created throughout an organization, the organization conditions itself to gradually enter the larger context of value-creation networks. These networks are based on complex alliances and relationships that link organizations to provide greater value to the customer than can be achieved in a simpler one-provider/one-customer relationship. An organization that has the architecture and infrastructure capabilities to develop and support effective communities of practice will be ideally placed to tap into the capabilities of others and take advantage of external partnership opportunities. They'll also recognize, and pay close attention to, the critical importance of ensuring the convergence of core values and generalized reciprocity. From this perspective, communities become essential components of the readiness required for competing in the emerging business environment of knowledge networks.

It's probable that communities of practice will grow in importance over the next few years, simply because they are ideal configurations for getting work done in the knowledge era. As conventional hierarchical structures and siloed functions increasingly become a barrier to effective working, organizations require new ways to conceptualize the organization-wide intersection of human and structural capital in the creation of customer and financial value.

Knowledge Network Mapping

A second knowledge exchange approach is knowledge network mapping. This methodology and supporting technology identifies and tracks the organization-wide exchange of knowledge. It visualizes and quantifies the effective connection routes and barriers to knowledge flow. Knetmap™, created by KonvergeandKnow, is a web-based data gathering and mapping software package that provides in-depth analysis of active networks and expertise of the organization.

The process of building a knowledge network map is quite simple. Members of the network to be mapped (the network may be an organization, department, team, interorganizational group, or even a subject or knowledge domain) are emailed a question, e.g., Whom do you contact to solve complex problems with Java technologies? or Whom do you contact for feedback on a new customer presentation?

An email hyperlink then takes the member answering the question to an online form that provides a list of internal and external people (or nodes as they are referred to on the map) to choose from. Members are also offered the opportunity to add a new external node. As answers are returned, a map of the organization is created (which typically starts to become visible within minutes of sending out the email). Each week the member is sent a further question until a particular dynamic (such as dealing with complex technological problems) is fully mapped.

A sample map is shown in Figure 9.3. To identify the knowledge centers (those sought for advice on this question), simply follow the arrows and look for the clusters in the knowledge-sharing networks.

By asking questions covering a range of subjects, it's possible over time to create a knowledge network map of the whole organization from a multitude of perspectives. By exposing these relationships, management can intervene and fine-tune them to make them more effective. Members engage in discussions about their organizational relationships and have specific conversations about how to improve their own personal effectiveness.

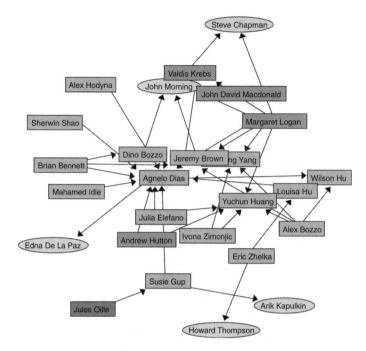

Figure 9.3 A Knowledge Network Map

A map will show not only exactly which people possess crucial knowledge but also how they share it. It will also identify people who may not be subject experts, but function as knowledge brokers— they're used to direct the enquirer to appropriate experts.

By examining various views or slices of the organization, Knetmap™ helps management to reveal:

- Informal leadership of the network
- Influencers on products, processes, services
- Product or process experts
- Which organizations influence the group
- Communities of practice or interest
- Fragmentation—who's not connected but should be
- Expertise or knowledge maps of a particular group
- Mentoring relationships—or lack thereof

- The conductivity of specific knowledge flows and movements in domain expertise over time
- Areas of risk for continuity plans.

Armstrong Case Example

As part of its knowledge strategy, Armstrong's senior management team concluded that improved management of tacit knowledge flows within the organization required someone to be responsible for knowledge, whom they call *knowledge stewards*. The knowledge stewards possess expert knowledge in their domain and also show a tendency to share that knowledge and partake in problem solving and innovation. They are described as lifelong learners who have the ability to communicate well with colleagues and promote the ideas of peers and colleagues.

Initially, the senior management team planned to select the top stewards for each knowledge domain. However, one employee suggested that, rather than making somewhat arbitrary choices, the organization should adopt a formal method of gathering data to confirm who the real knowledge stewards were. To meet this need, Armstrong implemented the Knetmap™ methodology.

Creating Knowledge Networks

All Armstrong employees, as well as employees from key business partners, were surveyed against a range of questions to map who went to whom for advice, expertise, opinion, guidance, or debate on the company's major knowledge domains (e.g., who was sought out for advice in developing new ideas or to discuss strategic initiatives). A knowledge network was mapped for each domain.

The next step was to use Knetmap™ to provide a deeper analysis. Knetmap™ uses a metric similar to Google™, which measures and ranks the links between web pages. Google™ gives more weight to incoming links from sites that themselves have a lot of incoming links. A social-network analysis measure called Prestige, which dates back to the 1950s, used a similar approach (2). Prestige ranked influencers and leaders in the medical community. A physician's Prestige measure was based on nomination by peers, and the measure increased if the nominators had high Prestige rankings themselves. Using Knetmap™ made it possible to see how knowledge was being shared throughout the organization and with its key partners.

Mapping Surprises

When the Armstrong knowledge network maps became visible, many managers were surprised at the results. The top ten list in each knowledge domain contained some expected names but also quite a few unexpected. Some experts were not on the lists, while some unexpected employees ranked high in a particular knowledge domain because the program doesn't merely evaluate expertise, it appraises an employee's ability and tendency to share knowledge and engage in problem solving and brainstorming.

Some experts, however knowledgeable, were not often asked for advice because they were seen as uncollaborative. Employees who functioned as brokers in the knowledge network, while not necessarily experts, ranked high in several knowledge domains. They had the exceptional ability to engage in a problem. Their problem-solving and interpersonal skills were top notch, and they knew where to find the experts. Other experts were discovered along the edge of the organization, well away from management's usual horizon of visibility. These were knowledgeable employees with a local reputation, local resources whom everyone around them utilized, but who weren't known organization-wide.

Figure 9.4 shows a network map for one knowledge domain. [Note that employees' names have been replaced by numbers to protect privacy.] The top three knowledge sources are nodes 17, 18, and 51. The first two were expected to be on the list, but 51 was a complete surprise to most, except to her immediate manager.

The network mapping process gives a clear understanding of the intensity with which employees transmit their knowledge throughout the organization and illustrates knowledge flows. It provides

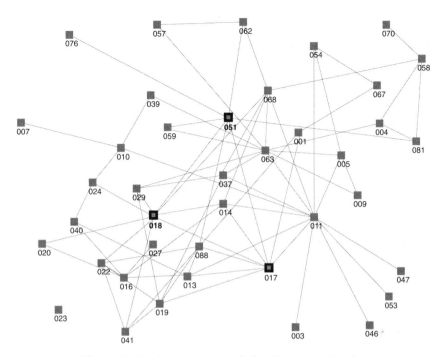

Figure 9.4   Armstrong Knowledge Domain Network

new employees or teams with an extremely useful artefact to access tacit knowledge that exists in the organization. More than anything, it serves as a useful metric of conductivity.

Knetmap^{TM} also produces an employee profile or yellow page for each person or node. The yellow pages list each employee's education, skills, current skill development program, project experience, current projects, aspirations, how they see themselves in the organizational context, and linked contact information. Additionally, they provide a hyperlink to the individual's knowledge artefact database.

Knowledge Artefacts

Artefacts are the explicit documented knowledge that each individual or group has contributed to the organizational knowledge pool.

Artefacts are the tangible things people create or use to help them get their work done (e.g., a written document is an artefact of what an individual or team knows, an organizational chart is an artefact created by the management team to describe the operational structure of the organization).

An artefact reveals the assumptions, concepts, strategy, and structure that guide the people who work with it. Understanding how artefacts are created and shared is an effective technique for visualizing the often hidden cultural principles governing knowledge creation and sharing within the organization.

The entry includes the context and/or background information on the artefact and the artefact itself. Each artefact is linked to other artefacts from which it was derived, to those employees who helped to create it, and to those who will likely make use of it.

A Knowledge Artefact Generator

Recognizing that people sometimes find it difficult to articulate what they know or to gauge its importance in an organizational context, Armstrong has experimented with what we call a Knowledge Artefact Generator. It's a multimedia tool designed to extract what employees know or have recently discovered for the purposes of sharing it with other employees. The Knowledge Artefact Generator contains guidelines for describing the artefact, referencing other artefacts, linking to historical artefacts, and tying artefacts to people, core competencies, and corporate strategy. The Knowledge Artefact Generator highlights four key elements:

- The importance of the artefact relative to strategic initiatives of the company
- The person or persons involved in creating the artefact
- A description of the artefact, using various tools and prompts to help an individual articulate what he or she knows, including metaphor, storytelling, and line of questioning, as well as different representations (drawings, audio clips, flowcharts)

■ Artefact Relationships—a file that identifies and links the artefacts that were drawn upon in some way to create the current artefact, artefacts that refer to the current artefact, and artefacts that were reused in some way to fashion the current artefact.

Artefact Network Maps

As with the organizational network maps above, the Knetmap™ methodology facilitates the creation of Artefact Network Maps, which can be analyzed to reveal:

■ Contributors to the organizational knowledge base
■ Artefacts that have a significant influence on the organization
■ Product/process experts
■ Areas of primary knowledge development in the organization
■ Areas of innovation in the organization
■ Strategic initiatives that are at the forefront of the organizational mind
■ Communities of practice or communities of interest.

The benefits of creating such a map include:

■ Directing the organization to explicit knowledge that should be shared and accessed more broadly
■ Using organizational expertise more effectively
■ Exposing employees' expertise and contributions to one another
■ Providing deeper meaning through making connections between artefacts
■ Encouraging innovation
■ Documenting relevant knowledge.

Knowledge Maps and Conventional Organizational Charts

With knowledge flows mapped and artefacts identified and continually created, knowledge maps illustrate the way work is really done within the organization. Flow mapping and artefact identification give a richer and more meaningful view of organizational dynamics than can be gleaned from a conventional organizational chart, which does not allow employees to see their ability to contribute to the organization as a whole. Moreover, organizational charts give no insight into the functioning of the team-based and cross-functional relationships that are the real drivers of innovation and competitive advantage in the knowledge era.

Knowledge Access and Learning

The second component of the knowledge architecture for the systems that generate capabilities is knowledge access. While learning (the process of turning information into knowledge for effective action) is also supported by knowledge exchange, we'll focus on how knowledge access, especially in the form of e-learning, enables this key capability generation system.

Learning takes place at four levels: individual, team, organizational, and customer, which, much like Russian matruschka dolls, are contained inside one another (see Figure 9.5). Learning at the individual level is found at the team level, which in turn is found at the organization level, which is found at the customer level. The individual level, the innermost kernel, is at the heart of the organization's ability to learn. In other words, a predisposition to learning on the part of individuals is a necessary condition for learning at the other levels.

For the conductive organization, continuous learning externally at the customer interface and internally across the organization begins with shaping the culture and creating the structural foundation so that an individual employee is ready, willing, and able to learn.

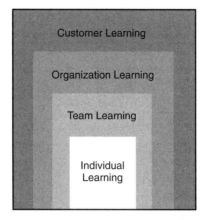

Figure 9.5 Levels of Learning

Learning and Work

A highly conductive organization creates an environment where learning is not just encouraged but perceived as virtually indistinguishable from working. The integration of work and learning is necessary because of the speed at which markets change. It's unrealistic for work and learning to travel separate trajectories or be seen as exclusive processes. If organizations are to be successful, the rate of learning must equal or exceed the rate at which markets change.

Learning, at all levels, must be recognized as so crucial to sustainable success that it becomes the organization's heartbeat. Armstrong's purpose statement is supported by two values that focus on generating capabilities: learning and innovation. Learning is also at the heart of Clarica's organizational structure, as shown in the following example.

Real-Time Learning at Clarica

Clarica created a multiwindow information system built to support customer service representatives in the organization's call center. When a customer calls, the service representative has a list of all the solutions purchased from the organization by this customer, details on their most recent transactions, the issues that were encountered, and how they were resolved. The full history of that customer is at the employee's fingertips.

Another window has the answers to any inquiry the customer might have. As customers ask their questions, the representatives can zero in on the corresponding logic trail and provide the best answer the organization can offer. Instead of training customer service representatives for months, Clarica enables representatives' self-initiated learning while interacting with the customer.

This example shows how real-time learning can help the employee work with the customer to find the right solution for that customer rather than offering the customer a standard set of answers about product offerings. It's also an example of how learning can be fully integrated with work. It's difficult to distinguish which part of this example should be characterized as work and which as learning.

Learning Purposes

Learning in a work context has two key purposes: enhancing and reframing. *Enhancing* is fine-tuning, deepening, and broadening capabilities within a given context and acquiring methods and rules for dealing with known and recurring situations. Enhancing continually improves existing systems and existing patterns of behavior and is essentially achieved through the harvesting of explicit knowledge. *Reframing* is the renewal of assumptions and beliefs to correspond more closely to the evolving reality of the marketplace and reinventing methods and approaches for dealing with new situations and challenges. Reframing leads to the development of new systems and patterns of behavior and is essentially achieved through the harvesting of tacit knowledge.

Self-Initiation

The first condition for effective learning is self-initiation. To guide decisions about the learning context, we've identified six principles:

- Learning is an employee expectation—every employee has the right to learn.
- Employees are responsible for their learning and for sharing their learning.
- Learning is integral to continuously improved business outcomes.
- Learning is best applied in the course of doing work.
- Technology should provide equitable access to learning opportunities as needed by the employee.
- Employees require opportunities to share and learn in groups.

As we can see, individual learning is the right of the individual, but employees are responsible for making sure learning happens and for sharing it organization-wide. Moreover, the organization must ensure that the conditions are right for learning to take place so that employees can access opportunities to increase their skills and knowledge as the need arises.

Learning Versus Training

Where self-initiation exists it's possible to replace traditional training approaches with alternative approaches. Enabling greater learning by eliminating a focus on training may seem paradoxical at a time when there is a growing need for knowledgeable employees. But traditional training approaches are increasingly found wanting as organizations attempt to keep pace with market demands. Training, which is usually delivered through classroom approaches out of the context of the work environment, cannot meet the just-in-time demand of a highly conductive organization.

With an instructor in control of the schedule, location, and content; the student a passive receiver of information out of context; and the experience counter to the culture and core values of the organization, there's little chance that capabilities can be generated.

To deal successfully with customers in the knowledge era, we must, more than ever before, have the necessary knowledge at our fingertips at all times. The capabilities of employees interacting with the customer must constantly be renewed and enhanced to meet ever-increasing customer requirements. Traditional training cannot begin to cope with the learning needs of people relating directly to customers.

In a learning as opposed to a training mode, we're operating not on the basis of the preparation and delivery of courses, but rather on creating a work environment in which employees can increase the specific competencies needed to perform their jobs (see Table 9.2).

e-Learning

With the principle of self-initiated learning established and the parallel paradigm shift from training to learning, it's critical to ensure that the infrastructure is in place to enable real-time, on-the-job learning. Leveraging web-enabled technologies and utilizing e-learning tools enable more effective learning. e-Learning is a networked approach to learning that is equally applicable to knowledge exchange and knowledge access.

Table 9.2   Distinctions between Training and Learning

Training	Learning
Prescriptive approach	Self-initiated approach
Led by instructor (push)	Self-directed (pull)
Mostly classroom-based	Multiple delivery
Delivering programs as an end	Increasing capability as an end
Participation is the only measurement	Demonstration of capability is the key measurement
Offered as one size fits all	Targets only the gap between required and current capability
Based on generic training needs analysis	Based on individual competency assessments

e-Learning should not be confused with e-training. All too often organizations automate their training and believe they are offering e-learning. As with traditional training and learning modes, the distinction between e-training and e-learning has to do with the delivery of knowledge—whether it is delivered via a push mode or a pull mode. The former is e-training, the latter is e-learning.

Web-Based Technologies

The proliferation of ways to connect with people and information is redefining how society and individuals behave, producing profound implications for how we organize, manage, lead, and elevate the performance of our organizations. Almost without exception, organizations today take advantage of web-enabled capabilities to share information. In a relatively short time, intranets have become an expected part of an organization's infrastructure. But intranets have been underutilized as real-time learning tools and as knowledge repositories. For the most part, intranets have become vast wastelands of static information.

Knowledge Depots

Clarica labelled its intranet Clarica Connects to emphasis access to tacit and explicit knowledge. Through the home page, employees could access information about business services, news, people services—even the cafeteria menu. It also included a Knowledge Depot that housed corporate policies and procedures, reference resources, and learning opportunities. It integrated work and learning resources in one place. The design made it possible to access information by resource type (e.g., a community of practice, course, learning module, policy, process, or procedure) or to enter a search string and view a list of all work-related information and learning opportunities within the organization as well as useful external links and references pertinent to that subject.

Knowledge Objects

From a learning perspective, when employees found knowledge they wished to explore, they could acquire knowledge by accessing units of knowledge, called *knowledge objects*—discrete units of knowledge that could be used on their own or assembled to create a more comprehensive resource. Working at the object level, it was easier to integrate quick references to support queries related to employee learning needs.

Learning centers were developed to automatically assemble knowledge objects to meet varying levels of learner needs on a particular subject—quick tips, brief overviews, learning modules, full courses, and links to experts and communities.

In the Leadership Learning Center, employees could search for learning opportunities and knowledge objects to develop their capabilities. For example, if someone had to provide feedback to a colleague and was unsure how to do it in the most constructive manner, the Leadership Learning Center could be accessed and searched under the phrase "giving feedback." A list of relevant resources was dynamically assembled, including: tips, links to policies, modules and courses on constructive performance feedback, and links to experts available to coach the employee on the specific situation.

Organization-Wide e-Learning

In the late 1990s Clarica purchased a large pension business from a bank and had to integrate the business into Clarica operations. Pension plans tend to be complex, so a conventional training approach would have required new employees to spend up to three months in the classroom to learn about Clarica's plans and platforms. This training would have been time-consuming and costly, and the delay in service frustrating to customers in the interim.

By deploying a knowledge-sharing system available at the desktop, a customer service representative servicing pension customers was able to ask a question relating to the pension process.

The question was either answered through an archived response or forwarded to an internal expert who handled that particular part of the plan. The expert's answer was supplied to the employee and then captured and archived to provide an automated response to a future enquiry.

Rather than employees' spending three months in a classroom being overloaded with information, most of which they either wouldn't retain or wouldn't ever use, this system provided the just-in-time learning that employees need.

Career Development

With a new employment contract that gives individuals the right and responsibility to develop their own capabilities, it's vital for organizations to ensure that employees have access to the best possible e-learning tools for capability and career development. At Clarica, all employees had their own I-Connect sections within the Clarica Connects portal that allowed them to manage their own capability and career development plans. I-Connect included a number of components:

- **Achievement Management**: Learn about achievement management. Create individual achievement plans and share the plans online with the employee's manager.
- **Learning and Development**: Access information and learn skills to assist with day-to-day work.
- **Career Management**: A complete framework for career management, from self-assessment to career options, effective job-search techniques, and job offer negotiations.

Career management provided employees with the ability to understand their work situation and create winning career strategies that align with their skills, desires, goals, and values and included personalized sections to assess: my fit with job opportunities, researching my career options, and taking action. It also included a self-management system that allowed employees to work through modules in areas such as: self-confidence, self-direction, and self-commitment. The self-confidence modules examined managing self-criticism, managing confidence through behavior, managing external criticism, managing change, and managing complacency.

Although we stress the importance of self-initiated learning, it's the organization's responsibility to make learning possible as a seamless, integrated process with work.

Conclusion

Systems to generate capabilities in the conductive organization must be fully aligned with the strategy, culture, and structures that support learning and collaborating that are seamlessly integrated with work. Industrial-era training can no longer meet the just-in-time need to generate capabilities at the speed that the market demands.

To fully leverage capability generation, the knowledge and learning system must be based on a comprehensive knowledge architecture that provides a blueprint for how knowledge can be accessed and exchanged from anywhere, but most importantly from the employee's desktop.

Knowledge and learning are at the core of capability generation. Tapping individual tacit knowledge and the collective explicit knowledge puts the wealth of an organization's most valuable asset in the hands of its employees and customers to create breakthrough performance.

Emerging Principles

■ Knowledge is the capability to take effective action.

■ Learning is the process of turning information into knowledge to take effective action.

- The systematic management of knowledge is fast becoming a strategic capability.

- Employees must assume responsibility for knowledge exchange as a key part of their learning and capability development—as part of the way they do their work.

- The rate of learning must equal or exceed the rate at which the marketplace changes.

- Enhancing learning continually improves existing systems and existing patterns of behavior.

- The first condition for effective learning is self-initiation.

- E-training is a push mode; e-learning is a pull mode.

- Knowledge and learning are at the core of capability generation.

References

1. Saint-Onge, H. and D. Wallace. (2003). *Leveraging Communities of Practice for Strategic Advantage.* Boston: Butterworth-Heinemann.
2. Wasserman, S. and K. Faoust. (1994). *Social Network Analysis, Methods and Applications.* Cambridge: Cambridge University Press.

10

A New Leadership Agenda for the Conductive Organization

Introduction

Leadership sits at the center of the organizational capability model for the conductive organization (see Figure 10.1). It triggers the dynamic tensions needed to keep the four key organizational capabilities calibrated to the customer. It synchronizes strategy, systems, structure, and culture—keeps them evolving to meet changing customer requirements. Leadership determines the bandwidth of knowledge flow, providing a catalyst for others to exercise their responsibilities, encouraging self-initiation, trust, interdependence, and partnering across the organization.

We define leadership as *the manner in which individuals choose to exercise their responsibilities*. We purposely use individuals and not managers because we see leadership as a capability that must be encouraged and nurtured within all employees, not just the few who sit at the top of the organizational chart. However, we also recognize that employees have varying degrees of leadership accountabilities. While everyone in the organization is encouraged to exercise their leadership capabilities in appropriate ways as dictated by customer needs, leadership at the senior and managerial levels has added accountabilities to set direction, manage performance, and make decisions that affect the dynamics of the organization.

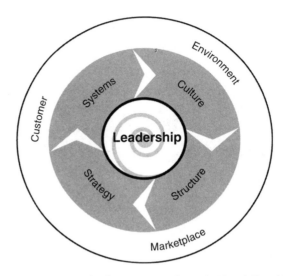

Figure 10.1   Leadership—A Core Organizational Capability

Leadership is an organizational capability. While individuals develop capabilities to better exercise their leadership, the organization creates the context for leadership. A person with highly developed leadership skills cannot exercise his or her leadership to its fullest in a nonsupportive context.

The leadership agenda outlined in this chapter is generic—applicable across industries, sectors, and corporate sizes. Although size affects some of the dynamics of leadership, the same fundamental issues remain for an organization of 500 or 50,000 people.

Leadership in the Industrial and Knowledge Eras

The leadership challenge today presents an exciting opportunity to transition organizational models from industrial-era to knowledge-era configurations. Testing new models and approaches is necessary to find an effective combination that will build a highly conductive organization. It's next to impossible to lead knowledge-era organizations with industrial-era structures and approaches. The differences in customer expectations alone are monumental.

In the industrial era, managers led through strict command and control structures. They were rewarded and promoted on the basis of their judicious allocation of scarce financial capital. The collective role of leadership was to successfully facilitate the process from making the product to selling it to customers. It was an inwardly focused leadership approach. Managers were not necessarily required to be customer-focused, and eliciting the commitment of their direct reports was far less important than making sure that their employees completed their narrowly defined tasks. This approach was the norm for almost two hundred years.

Working with organizations transitioning from industrial-era to knowledge-era paradigms, we've observed that successful leadership operates not through an internal pyramid but through the assembly, disassembly, and reassembly of cross-disciplinary teams, which may also include customers and/or partners. Leaders are able to foster an environment of learning, trust, and collaboration in which values-based relationships are built with customers and employees are committed to the organization's vision. To accomplish these goals, we need a new leadership agenda—new forms of leadership mindsets, values, and competencies.

Organizations today are based on radically different assumptions than were historically used (see Table 10.1). These changes in focus have resulted in new meaning for the leadership agenda (see Table 10.2).

As these tables illustrate, the required leadership approaches today are conceptually and practically far removed from much we've seen before. A key difference is that knowledge-era organizational assumptions start with the customer and challenge the leadership dynamic to constantly calibrate the organizational capabilities to customer needs.

Table 10.1 Industrial-Era and Knowledge-Era Organizational Assumptions

Industrial Era Assumptiomns	Knowledge Era Assumptions
Production/ Product/ Marketing Customer Resource Services	Customer Team Resources Solutions
Divide and subdivide work for greater efficiency	Cluster capabilities in cross-disciplinary teams
Prosper by focusing on one's own interests in a win-lose competitive context	Complement one's own values and capabilities with those of others in a win-win context both within and between companies
Create value by transforming raw matter into finished goods	Create value by building on ideas, including those of customers and uppliers
Optimize capital assets by managing associated costs	Leverage both capital and knowledge assets
Lead through hierarchical command and control approach	Lead by fostering values and a culture based on interdependence

A New Model of Leadership

Starting with customers and working back toward the organization—an *outside-in* perspective—means new challenges for the leadership agenda. To summarize the sequence:

- In the knowledge era success begins by defining the relationship that the organization wishes to develop with customers and the relationship that customers wish to develop with the organization.
- Based on this customer focus is a need to identify and nurture the type of culture that will deliver to this customer relationship.
- Culture becomes an organizational capability by describing and living a set of shared or core values that are also aligned to the values of the customer.
- Articulate the type of leadership capability that is required to engender a values-based, customer-calibrated culture—with

emphasis on self-initiation, trust, interdependence, and part-nering characteristics.

Table 10.2 Leadership Approaches in the Industrial and Knowledge Eras

Industrial Era Leadership Approaches	Knowledge Era Leadership Approaches
Compartmentalize functions and tasks in a command and control context	Minimize "organizational walls" in order to optimize the ability to exploit rapidly and unpredictably changing market opportunities Provide quick access to total skills base of the organization
Establish lines of control through hierarchical structures	Manage accountabilities through a shared sense of responsibility Enable team/re-team to provide the routine reconfiguration of resources dedicated to a particular customer's needs
Define closely supervised rules and procedures to limit freedom of manoeuvre in order to ensure performance standards	Purposefully generate knowledge and expertise Reward value-adding contribution through teams

Given that we view leadership as an organizational capability as much as the competence of any one person, we believe that leader-ship must become a core competence of the organization, a critical component of its structural capital. The leadership capabilities we describe serve as both required attributes of corporate leaders and descriptors of what may help organizations assume a leadership position in their industries. The capabilities can be seen as much as descriptors of the conductive organization as of an individual exer-cising his or her leadership.

We've identified five capabilities that we've found useful in build-ing a leadership profile needed in the knowledge era. The profile outlines an ideal, an aspirational level that we can work toward. Very few individuals will embody all of these attributes. The challenge is

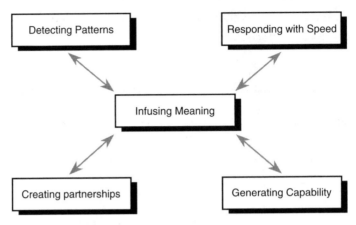

Figure 10.2 Leadership Capability Model

to begin building these capabilities at all levels of the organization and ensure that, at senior leadership levels, a team collectively possesses these characteristics.

The core leadership capabilities required in a highly conductive organization include: detecting patterns, responding with speed, creating partnerships, generating capability, and infusing meaning (see Figure 10.2). Note that infusing meaning sits at the center of the model. Like leadership's position in the model of key organizational capabilities, infusing meaning enables a leader to orchestrate and effectively deploy the other four capabilities.

Detecting Patterns

To detect patterns, people need to:

- Understand the dynamics of the marketplace
- Isolate and interpret trends
- Assess the response patterns of the organization
- Track the expectation/capability ratio.

We know that markets shift rapidly today, and that customers are demanding more value-added components in their relationships with suppliers. Detecting patterns requires a sense-and-respond mindset across the organization. Sensing and responding may be achieved through something as complex in practice as the unfiltered mindsets approach adopted by Mayekawa Manufacturing or something as simple as the following approach used by a fast-food chain in Tennessee:

At Pal's Sudden Service, winner of a Malcolm Baldrige National Quality Award in 2001, leadership team members must knock on doors within the vicinity of their restaurants, seeking direct input on customer satisfaction and preferences. The introduction of flavored drinks was one innovation resulting from this practice. As for financial payback, in 2001 when competitors had flat revenues, Pal's increased sales by 21% without price increases. (2)

The leadership team at Pal's Sudden Service not only required good communication skills and an ability to represent their brand promise to customers, they required the analytical skills to understand the implications of what was happening in their markets—they needed to be able to recognize patterns and then have the courage to make strategic decisions based on their analysis and insights.

If leaders cannot perceive the business environment accurately and cannot respond accordingly, they will risk the danger of moving at the last minute and making decisions that are inspired by panic, increasing the likelihood of strategic failure.

Responding with Speed

To respond to market forces in a timely manner requires:

- Compressing timeframes for decision-making/execution
- Instilling a collective sense of urgency
- Configuring and reconfiguring capabilities and business processes
- Sharing information quickly and openly.

With most markets today propelled at warp speed, it's incumbent on organizations to ensure that the rate of decision making and implementation are equally rapid. Clearly, protracted decision making processes negate any notion of speed. To become highly conductive, an organization must remove unnecessary barriers to decision-making and make valid information available to enable people to make accurate assumptions. Conductivity has both quality and transmission components—leaders must ensure that the high-quality information is available and accessible.

A shared vision reduces the time frame of achieving goals. At Armstrong, our shared vision is outlined in our purpose statement:

We are committed to developing and facilitating new capabilities for our worldwide customers and ourselves.

This shared vision creates a common understanding about what the organization is trying to achieve. It provides a laser focus for our decision-making process.

Supporting this vision is alignment to core values, the criteria for all decisions, actions, and behaviors. For example, Armstrong has a value focused on learning and innovating with customers. Any idea or suggestion that may create capabilities through innovating with customers will be approved without lengthy debate and can be initiated at any level without going through management hierarchy.

The ability to configure and reconfigure business processes and capabilities, to continually calibrate to the customer, is central to the leadership agenda today. It requires that the leadership team understands the big picture of how their organization is working in relation to the customer needs, an ability to orchestrate high-level changes to business processes, and an ability see where new or evolved capabilities are required. At the operational level, an understanding of how capabilities can best be configured for specific projects and an ability to ensure that project teams work cohesively are required.

Creating Partnerships

The ability to create partnerships includes:

- Interacting intensively with customers to craft opportunities
- Building alliances and coalitions in the marketplace
- Forming and reforming teams across functions and with customers
- Collaborating to actively manage interdependencies.

The capability to effectively manage complex partnerships is growing in importance as organizations are reconfigured. Organizations are becoming more and more involved in complex value-creation networks, where the boundaries between one organization and another become blurred and functions are integrated. It's becoming a critical organizational and leadership capability to be able to create and leverage participation in network-designed and -delivered solutions. Trust fosters this commitment and cements the network partnership. By forming value-creation networks focused on fulfilling customer requirements (see Figure 10.3), true customer calibration can be accomplished.

Leaders articulate the common objectives and values to which the network commits and around which it can coalesce. Control must be replaced by empowerment through self-initiation, with the network members being given the freedom to find the most appropriate route to achieve project goals.

The network will be held accountable for delivering its objectives. Leadership's responsibility is to ensure that systems and structures are in place that enable the members of the network to collaborate, learn, share knowledge, and execute their responsibilities. The network's output is the generation of capabilities.

Generating Capabilities

In order to generate the capabilities on which the organization depends for its growth in the marketplace, leadership must engender:

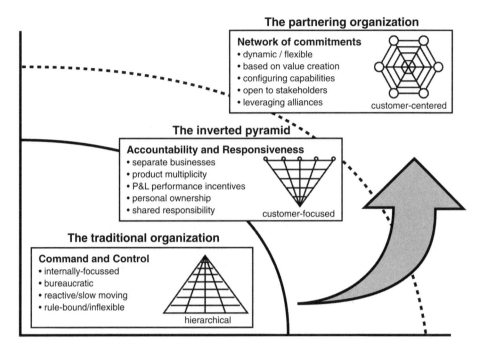

Figure 10.3 Working Toward the Partnering Organization

- A focus on developing core competencies based on customer needs
- Continuous learning to enhance competencies on a just-in-time basis
- Learning from experience at individual and organizational levels
- Aligning/re-aligning of capabilities for optimal performance.

Generating capabilities in real time at the speed that the market requires is a key component of the leadership agenda. Understanding customer aspirations and creating the capabilities to service customers' articulated and unarticulated needs requires a special set of generative capabilities—learning, collaborating, and strategy-making.

Learning from experience at individual and organizational levels is an extremely rich form of learning in that it is contextual and reflects what worked and what didn't work. Employees must feel confident that they can be open about sharing what they, in all good faith, tried but found didn't work. Failures can be seen as prized knowledge assets from which to learn. They need to be captured and codified or shared as part of the knowledge flow. Innovation cannot take place without failure. Leaders should develop the confidence to see failures as the foundation stones for future success. It's incumbent on leadership to ensure that generating capabilities through a wide range of channels is encouraged and made available across the organization with equitable access to all employees.

Infusing Meaning

To infuse meaning in an organization requires that leaders:

- Foster an ongoing strategic dialogue, including customers
- Make meaning from the business context
- Instill a shared vision and sense of purpose
- Develop strategic agendas with collective ownership
- Adopt "stretch" goals to leverage resources through innovation
- Strike values-based alignment with customers
- Provide focus to people who are knowledgeable, flexible, and empowered.

Leadership is responsible for both being aware of and understanding its marketplace, for interpreting patterns internally and externally, and for aligning organizational capabilities accordingly. In addition, leadership is responsible for creating awareness about directions—for communicating that the organization does understand what's happening in the marketplace and how this understanding guides strategic direction. Leaders of great organizations learn how to articulate the purpose, or meaning, of their corporations in ways that transcend everyday business constructs and inspire all who come into contact with the corporation.

The ability to make sense, to create meaning, requires the adoption of a collegial style of leadership. At Armstrong, there are regular context-setting meetings where management comes together to explore and question the context in and concepts by which the organization operates. In these meetings, managers know that their views are sought and appreciated and will serve as the basis for inquiry and action. This process is only possible within a healthy leadership environment.

In the central role of the leadership model, infusing meaning suggests that leadership will encourage the organization to stretch to outperform its competitors. An important leadership capability is assessing the situation and adjusting the stretch limit to an acceptable and comfortable level.

These five leadership capabilities translate into ten leadership qualities:

- Being market-focused
- Being customer-calibrated
- Sensing and responding
- Ensuring knowledge flows are as wide as possible
- Configuring and reconfiguring customer-focused processes and capabilities
- Making rapid decisions
- Building high-trust partnerships internally and externally
- Continuously learning
- Focusing strategically
- Making meaning.

Broad-Based Leadership

At the beginning of this chapter, we suggested that leadership is an organizational capability that must permeate the organization. Leadership is also an individual capability that should be developed in all employees—not just a select few at the top of the organizational chart. However, many organizations demoralize their employees by focusing leadership development on a small cadre of *high potentials.* In a corporation of 50,000, there's a danger that this practice sends out a message that says we have 300 eagles and 49,700 turkeys. It's saying that these people are the ones we're interested in and the rest are not. This practice works against establishing a culture of self-initiation and creates a barrier to knowledge flow.

Of course organizations need to pay attention to developing tomorrow's senior leaders, but it's not effective to create leadership development programs with such a narrow focus. Rather, all employees should be encouraged and enabled to develop their leadership skills for their own benefit and in congruence with the requisite leadership behaviors of the organization. Development of leadership capabilities also requires a knowledge infrastructure, a system that helps employees understand and practice leadership skills as they relate to their everyday work.

A concept we've found useful in coalescing self-initiation with leadership skills is *broad-based leadership.* One way of describing broad-based leadership is to consider a group of people who are working as a team. If there is a culture of self-initiation, employees will assume responsibility for their own individual performance and capabilities. They'll also be expected, in partnership with their colleagues, to assume shared responsibility for running the part of the business for which that team is accountable. Their commitment to create value for the organization in return for being able to create capabilities for themselves is at the heart of the new commitment-based contracts.

The designated team leader is the person we describe as the first among equals. With teams being continually configured and reconfigured, different people are called upon at different times to assume first-among-equals status. The team leader works as a member of the team, but has a veto right based on his or her responsibility to the next level of management. It's this person's job not to command and control but to engender an environment of high trust in which employees are willing to work in partnership to build on one another's capabilities for their own benefit and that of the team,

The traditional model

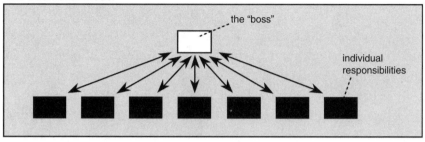

The team leadership model

Figure 10.4 Comparison of Leadership Models

organization, and customer. It's the team leader's responsibility to ensure that the localized valves regulating knowledge flows are opened fully. This new leadership model differs significantly from a traditional model (see Figure 10.4). Our thinking in this area has, in large part, been guided by Russell Ackoff's work. (1)

This new leadership model can be seen at a Michigan-based natural resources company, CMS Energy Corporation (see Table 10.3). They restated their view of leadership as part of a corporate change exercise. They recognized that their leadership paradigms were partly responsible for poor financial performance.

Values-Based Leadership

The effectiveness and development of leaders at every level of the organization can be tracked through a values instrument. Ensuring that leaders exercise their responsibilities according to a

Table 10.3 Leadership Paradigm Shift at CMS Energy Corporation

Old Line Beliefs About Leadership	New Philosophy of Leadership
Only a certain few people are born to lead and the corporate challenge is to identify them early. After that, the company should make every effort to retain them and further their careers so they can rise to the top of the organizational hierarchy where they belong	Many people can learn to lead quite well. It is a question of identifying their distinct leadership strengths and weaknesses and then systematically developing their potential to its fullest, i.e., "leaders are made and not born"
A leader who is good for one specific situation or successful at a certain time will also be just as effective in most other situations and circumstances. I.e., "once a leader always a leader"	Leadership is highly situational, with a leader's effectiveness depending on the best fit between an individual's talents, followers' needs, and the specific challenges/conditions of the situation
Leaders should be self-selected through internal competition, where succession becomes a survival of the fittest contest	Some leaders are good leaders for one time and place but they could be ineffective in another time and place—leadership should rotate as circumstances change
Only a leader can spot leadership potential, so leaders should pick their successors	As leadership potential is impossible to spot, organizations need to invest in developing a larger leadership talent bench from which future leaders can be selected as conditions and circumstances dictate
Leaders are the most critical members of the workforce and contribute most to corporate success. The effort to retain, richly reward, and generally pamper top leaders is justified by their great value to the bottom line	Good leaders are not even a condition for corporate success—rather they are an enabling variable for organizational effectiveness. Leadership is not a sufficient condition for corporate profitability since a chain is only as good as its weakest link. Therefore, general talent development is more important than leadership development to improve corporate performance
20% of employees at the top of the hierarchy matter most. The 70% of employees who are followers are highly replaceable. The other 10% are bottom-dwellers needing to be systematically culled from the workplace and replaced.	The rewards of success should be spread more broadly across all contributors and more equally between followers who do the work and leaders who only facilitate that work.

Reprinted with permission from High Performance Leadership, *CRF Publishing, London, UK, 2003, Chris Ashton & Andrew Lambert.*

well-described set of core values, with supporting leadership behaviors is a key requirement for building values-based conductive organizations.

In recent years we've seen how the behavior of leaders can fatally damage an organization, even one that has historically been seen as a great organization. It's not just a matter of managing the risk of strategic failure. Fundamentally, an organization does all that it can to ensure that it's not vulnerable to destruction by unethical leaders. A set of leadership values that are non-negotiable is key for mitigating this risk. The organization must make it clear that, if leaders do not live by these values, they cannot and will not be allowed to hold leadership positions at any level.

The power of leadership values is that they instill a well-defined and understood set of leadership accountabilities. Without this level of accountability, organizations are prone to corruption. When leadership values and behaviors are culturally protected, contradictory behavior is quickly identified because the leadership principles have been collectively adopted, agreed upon, and institutionalized.

Clarica's three core values (partnership, stewardship, and innovation) were translated into 18 leadership behaviors. Although these behaviors were embraced and lived by the executive team, they were also expected from all employees across the organization. The leadership behaviors were described in action-oriented terms to stress that employees should be proactive in bringing these values to life:

Partnership in action:
- Seek and build partnerships
- Listen and understand
- Communicate clearly and honestly
- Foster collaboration
- Encourage the heart
- Appreciate diversity

Stewardship in action:
- Act with integrity
- Look outward

- Optimize customer success
- Act with energy to get results
- Be a leader
- Take ownership

Innovation in action:
- Be entrepreneurial
- Be solutions-oriented
- Commit to learning
- Actively request and offer feedback
- Take risks to meet the vision
- Create and share knowledge.

Monitoring leadership values and behaviors is an ongoing process where assessment is used as the basis for interventions focused on evolving behaviors towards an ideal state. This monitoring and assessment can be achieved through a values system.

Clarica's quarterly Values of Your Voice survey completed by employees monitored how leadership values and behaviors were being lived. Employees were asked whether they agreed, somewhat agreed, somewhat disagreed, or disagreed with 100 statements designed to discover how the employee experienced the culture of the organization. Leadership-oriented statements included:

- Strategic direction is clear, vision is meaningful. I know how I contribute.
- My manager expects collaboration.
- People are empowered, trust one another, and take risks.
- Poor performance is managed effectively.

From the survey findings, Clarica's executive team had one view of how individuals were developing requisite leadership values and behaviors and another of how this development was experienced by the employee-base.

The Dangers of Managing through the Spreadsheet

Without anchoring leadership capabilities and expected behavior in values, an organization can fall into a number of habits that are detrimental to conductivity. A key danger is a view of the organization only through the eye of the spreadsheet. We aren't in any way questioning the need for strong financial discipline or prudence, but rather highlighting the inherent risk of such an approach.

Senior leaders who make decisions based only on what spreadsheet cells tell them may behave contrary to the organization's best interest. For instance, to get the right numbers, funding may have to be pulled from initiatives (e.g., lay-off people, discontinue learning resources, reduce travel) that build capabilities or deepen relationships. Such a move may provide short-term financial success and may even be applauded by the markets, but it carries a long-term cost as capabilities and relationships disintegrate.

Leaders with a spreadsheet mindset run the risk of sending mixed messages through the organization that can wreak cultural havoc and lead to employee disengagement. For example, a CEO may say "our people are our most valuable asset" and then say "80 per cent of expense is people and so to achieve an ROE (return on equity) of X percent we have to cut Y number of people." What this leader is doing is saying in one breath that people are indispensable to the value proposition of the business and in the next that they are totally dispensable.

We aren't saying that downsizing must be avoided at all costs. Of course, there are times when it's a required organizational response to changing market demands or a result of technological enhancement or a merger. What we're saying is that it should be deployed judiciously and appropriately.

Removing Fear

The constant threat of downsizing will naturally engender fear in individuals. Where fear predominates, people will hide mistakes, not take risks, and become competitive with their colleagues. Considered from a values perspective, they'll more likely operate through the basic and narrower values related to survival rather than values that promote greater interdependence and partnership. In a climate of fear, employees are incapable of entering into a high-trust relationship with customers. We cannot expect employees to own their relationship with the customer and open up to customers' concerns with care and attention when the organization doesn't enter into high-trust relationships with employees—where care and attention are equally evident.

The Importance of Integrity

One of the most important mandates of knowledge-era leaders is to ensure that a very high level of trust is maintained within all the organization's relationships. At the same time an environment where people are willing to change rapidly on a regular basis must be created. If the level of trust is eroded by the way leadership functions, there will be a build-up of resistance to change as employees stop believing in the organization's goals and adjust their commitment accordingly. Basically, leading with integrity (2) means that we stand for what we believe.

Consequently, it's incumbent on leaders to have the courage to act with integrity even when tough and unpopular decisions must be made. When Clarica purchased the Canadian operations of MetLife, a significant number of staff lost their jobs. Clarica endeavored to work through the layoffs with a high degree of integrity. Difficult communications about job status were delivered in an honest, straightforward manner. Clarica made the commitment that all former MetLife staff would know within six weeks of the merger whether or not there would be a role for them going forward. Acting with integrity creates a platform for delegating responsibility, encouraging self-initiation, and increasing trust. It's the way to encourage people to exercise a higher degree of leadership in a conductive organization.

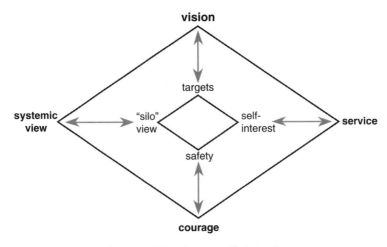

Figure 10.5 Acting with Integrity

Leadership integrity has been illustrated by Koestenbaum as a diamond linking four key elements: vision, service, courage, and systemic view (see Figure 10.5). (3) When leadership integrity becomes eroded in an organization, behaviors revert to the inner diamond (self-interest, safety, silo view, and targets). Instead of striving to realize a worthwhile vision, leaders place single-minded importance on targets that become devoid of meaning.

A healthy organization and its leaders are at the service of a worthwhile cause. This is lost when leaders become self-serving. This behavior has a disproportionate impact on depleting the trust reservoir of the organization. When everyone starts looking out for themselves as individuals, the organization loses its coherence and the outside-in perspective becomes clouded.

Self-serving behaviors also lead directly to an erosion of courage to safety. When leaders no longer stand for what they believe, they take refuge in safe behaviors. At this point, they generally have *quit and stayed*—they're there in body, but little else. From this perspective, it's not possible to care for the collective success of the organization. It's a contagious condition. Everyone starts marking time and optimizing their own narrow, individual interests. Leaders lose their systemic, holistic view and no longer act in the organization's collective interest. The inner diamond takes on a centrifugal dynamic of its own where the erosion of one dimension leads to the erosion of the next. This illustration can provide identification of symptoms that point to the start of erosion. At any point, an organization's climate can be mapped onto the arrows that link the outer diamond to the inner diamond. With the tension between these two diamonds in mind, leaders can easily monitor the overall climate of leadership integrity that characterizes their organization.

Conclusion

A new leadership agenda, based on core values, is needed in a highly conductive organization. Recognition that all employees have a mandate to exercise their leadership capabilities moves the organization to a self-initiated culture that has the capabilities to create and maintain high-trust relationships both internally and externally.

As an organizational capability, leadership is the dynamic that provides the tension to constantly calibrate the four core capabilities—to keep the organization focused on an outside-in perspective. Traditional leadership styles and attitudes toward leadership development are rapidly changing in the knowledge era. Organizations that recognize the need to move to a new leadership agenda are creating environments in which leadership capabilities can be exercised by all employees—no matter where they sit in the organizational structure.

Emerging Principles

- Leadership is a capability that must be encouraged and nurtured within all employees, not just the few who sit at the top of the organization chart.

- The ability to configure and reconfigure business processes and capabilities, to continually calibrate to the customer, is central to the leadership agenda today.

- Leadership's responsibility is to ensure that systems and structures are in place to enable members of a value-creation network to collaborate, learn, share knowledge, and execute their responsibilities.

- Recognition that all employees have a mandate to exercise their leadership capabilities moves the organization to a self-initiated culture that has the capabilities to create and maintain high-trust relationships both internally and externally.

- A set of leadership values that are non-negotiable is key for mitigating governance risk.

- Where fear predominates, people will hide mistakes, not take risks, and become competitive with their colleagues.

- It's becoming a critical organizational and leadership capability to be able to create and leverage participation in network-designed and -delivered solutions.

- Leadership operates through the assembly, disassembly, and reassembly of cross-disciplinary teams, which may also include customers and/or partners.

- Understanding customer aspirations and creating the capabilities to service customers' articulated and unarticulated needs requires a special set of generative capabilities—learning, collaborating, and strategy making.

- Great organizations learn how to articulate the purpose, or meaning, of their corporations in ways that transcend everyday business constructs and inspire all who come into contact with the corporation.

- All employees should be encouraged and enabled to develop their leadership skills for their own benefit and in congruence with the requisite leadership behaviors of the organization.

- When leadership values and behaviors are culturally protected, contradictory behavior is quickly identified because the leadership principles have been collected, adopted, agreed upon, and institutionalized.

- Senior leaders who make decisions based only on what spreadsheet cells tell them may behave contrary to the organization's best interest.

- In a climate of fear employees will be incapable of entering into a high-trust relationship with customers.

- If the level of trust is eroded by the way leadership functions, there will be a build-up of resistance to change as employees stop believing in the organization's goals and adjust their commitment accordingly.

References

1. For more information on Russell Ackoff's work see:
   Ackoff, R.L. (1994). *The Democratic Corporation: A Radical Prescription for Recreating Corporate America and Rediscovering Success.* New York: Oxford University Press.
   Ackoff, R.L. (1999). *Re-Creating the Corporation: A Design of Organization for the 21st Century.* New York: Oxford University Press.
2. For more information on leadership integrity, see Barbara Annis's work at http://www.baainc.com
3. Koestenbaum, P. (1991). *Leadership: The Inner Side of Greatness.* San Francisco: Jossey-Bass.

11

From Conductive to Highly Conductive—The Evolving Organization

Introduction

An alternate title for this concluding chapter might have been "A Work in Progress—The Never-Ending Journey to a Highly Conductive State." As we outlined in the first chapter, we've by no stretch of the imagination come to a definitive answer about how a conductive organization should be structured—what's going to be the answer for the ever-emerging challenges of the knowledge era. Instead, we've offered our opinion as to where we should be headed, based on reflection on our own experiences in practice, as well as our conversations with colleagues and peers.

In a keynote address to delegates at the May 2003 Knowledge Nets Conference in New York City, knowledge visionary Larry Prusak talked about ideas and the endless trail of supposed leading-edge approaches that organizations worldwide keep experimenting with in hopes of finding a winning combination. He suggested that the reason so many ideas come and go is that business management is an art, not a science—there are no proven principles, theorems, and laws to guide decisions. As a result, we continue to work with the raw materials that we have, trying new approaches and combinations to create an ever-hopeful masterpiece.

We started by setting a context for the highly conductive organization and outlining why we think it's important to pay attention to the changes around us. We continued by outlining two overarching frameworks that guide our thinking—The Knowledge Capital Model and the customer-calibration perspective. The main body of this book describes the four key organizational capabilities (strategy, culture, structure, and systems) and how a new leadership agenda functions to synchronize these components with customer needs. And now, we end our work by turning the spotlight back on you to think about how the characteristics of a highly conductive organization can be applied to your organization, using the questions at the end of this chapter.

The Power of the Customer

During our journey of discovery we've witnessed, as most practitioners have, a seemingly unstoppable upward trajectory of customer requirements and expectations as they take fuller advantage of the choices, opportunities, and connectivity of the digital age. Over the next few years, power will become even more concentrated in the hands of the customer. The days when suppliers called the shots belong to the diaries and history books of the last millennium.

In the digital age or the knowledge era, customer satisfaction and customer loyalty carry little weight as isolated measures of supposed success. The key to success lies in the capability to calibrate to the customer—a capability that includes constant focusing and refocusing of the organization, adjusting to the customer's ever-rising standards.

Panning for Knowledge

Learning and collaborating with the customer is becoming a required capability of all organizations. These generative capabilities enable higher levels of conductivity, beginning at the customer interface and spreading throughout the organization. Without this conductivity, the organization's competitive position will quickly atrophy as other, more nimble corporations find the solutions that customers are seeking and calibrate themselves accordingly.

Learning and collaboration are prerequisite processes, part of the systems organizational capability, for turning the information gathered from the external environment into strategically valuable knowledge within the organization. We don't need a crystal ball to predict that the amount of information generated will balloon to an unimaginable size in the next few years.

The rules of business are changing. In the industrial era, value lay in tangible commodities such as gold. Its value was based on its rarity. In the knowledge era, the most valuable commodity, information, is less tangible, but it is abundant. The trick for successful organizations is to pan the golden nuggets of knowledge from the fast-flowing rivers of information. Conductivity is as much about the quality of the knowledge transmitted within the conductive organization as it is about the speed of transmission.

The Role of Employees

Just as we've witnessed a transformation in how we relate to the customer, we're also experiencing a reappraisal of how organizations relate to their employees. We're rethinking the role of employees as we reconfigure our organizations.

We've emphasized the need for customer calibration, high-trust cultures, and partnership networks. These dimensions all rely on self-initiated employees working in an enabling culture who take responsibility for expanding the bandwidth and increasing the quality of conductivity within their organizations.

One of our greatest challenges is bringing employees to assume self-initiation. It takes a concerted effort to create the organizational context for self-initiation. While most organizations claim to have transcended an entitlement or dependency orientation, in reality, much work remains to be done to move toward a culture of self-initiation for all employees, including those with senior-level management responsibilities.

As we move deeper into the knowledge era, a new reality is dawning. Individuals are taking responsibility for creating their own knowledge from the mass of information available by joining virtual networks of like-minded people around the globe. What's more, they are learning how to work these networks for maximum knowledge creation, largely by figuring out how to deepen relationships, across time and space, with their networked partners.

A challenge for organizations in the future is how to harness the learning and collaboration skills of such individuals to the benefit of the organization and its customers. As a younger, more Internet-savvy generation joins the workforce, more and more individuals come to the workplace with these new skills already honed. It's unlikely that these individuals will commit to an organization unless they can utilize these skills as an everyday part of their job. Leaders will need to develop the capabilities to enable this new level of knowledge-creation and networking capability—to encourage it to operate unimpeded, while being able to channel and make meaning of the mass of knowledge and complexity of relationships generated.

A New Leadership Agenda

We've focused a great deal of attention on the need for a new leadership agenda. There's little doubt that the capabilities and qualities of an accomplished leader are being redefined and will continue to evolve. Leading a customer-calibrated, networked organization bears little resemblance to leading a traditional, industrial-era structured hierarchy.

As leaders, we are all charged with finding the most appropriate and effective way to configure our organizations to achieve sustainable success. It's unquestionably *the* great leadership challenge in the knowledge era.

The possible sociotechnical configurations of organizations are many and still evolving. What the template for the high-performing organization of tomorrow will look like we cannot fully predict. In all probability, there won't be a standard textbook approach. What is certain is that the successful approaches that emerge will, to a substantial degree, be dependent on the integration of technology-enabled collaboration and learning mechanisms with organizational structures. Unimpeded collaboration and learning, supported by technology, will enable employees to systematically harvest and apply new knowledge.

The Conductive Organization

Within the conductive organization, we've described one possible sociotechnical configuration based on four core organizational capabilities (strategy, culture, structure, and systems) synchronized in a dynamic way by leadership (see Figure 11.1). In the final analysis, we haven't evolved our thinking and approaches as an academic exercise, no matter how intellectually challenging and rewarding we're finding the journey. We recognized the urgency for finding new ways to lead our corporations to sustainable success. Given the

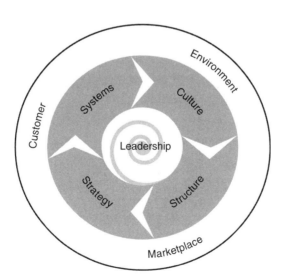

Figure 11.1 Organizational Capability Model for the Conductive Organization

warp speed at which our social and market environments are changing and how it affects people's behavior, it seems inconceivable to us that organizations that continue to operate by the old rules will survive into the future.

In evolving our thinking, we didn't simply jettison all that we've learned from our past experience. We certainly didn't destroy the historic cultural foundations on which our organizations were built. What we did do was recalibrate for a new reality—a recalibration that will continue to take place as we take the next step on our path to a higher state of conductivity.

Turning the Spotlight

Although every organization has its unique characteristics, they all have similar foundations. Our challenge to you is to take the time to analyze the current state of your organization by answering the following questions. Your reflection should help you either start or continue your own journey toward an organization that functions at a higher level of conductivity—that can achieve breakthrough performance and sustainable success.

1. **What strategic risks may be mitigated by becoming a more highly conductive organization?**

At the outset it's well worth articulating the ways in which your organization would benefit from becoming more conductive. What performance challenges could be more effectively addressed with increased speed and quality of knowledge flow? Given the large-scale transformation of external and internal structures and mindsets that are required for enhanced conductivity, the challenges will typically be strategic in nature. Becoming more conductive will help mitigate the prospect of strategic failure—failure that may be the result of an inability to read markets, a slowness to respond, disconnection from customers, unpreparedness of employees, or loss of trust and reputation.

Key questions to ask are:

- How will becoming more conductive increase our chances of successfully executing strategies?
- Which strategic or organizational risk factors can be identified and how will they be managed?

At the beginning of the journey, it's worth knowing how your organization will benefit from becoming more highly conductive. Identifying the strategic imperative of high-quality knowledge flow is the first step in recognizing the need to move toward a higher state of conductivity.

2. Assess your organization, business unit, or team against our definition of the conductive organization.

We define the conductive organization as:

An organization that continuously generates and renews capabilities to achieve breakthrough performance by enhancing the quality and the flow of knowledge and by calibrating its strategy, culture, structure, and systems to the needs of its customers and the marketplace.

Moving toward a more conductive level requires parallel efforts to create and enhance the capability-building and relationship-deepening approaches we've described. It's beneficial to assess the gap between your current organizational state and your desired future state.

Consider these questions:

- How close are we to achieving unimpeded knowledge flows and where are the major barriers?
- How effective are we at learning? How do we learn with and about our customers? What are the barriers to learning? What opportunities are there to leverage our technology to enable

continuous learning? How do we put our new knowledge to work?

- How effective are we at generating new capabilities in real time, calibrated to the customer?
- Do we practice internally what we need to apply externally?
- How do we measure what we've achieved?
- How capable are we of high and sustainable performance?

By taking time to step back and identify the major barriers to becoming a more highly conductive organization, you will get a sense of the gap and the challenges ahead. You may also be able to identify where early interventions can be applied—the quick wins that motivate continued improvement.

3. What would a highly conductive organization look like from your customers' perspective?

Step outside your organization and view it through the eyes of your customer. Look at it as it is and then as it could be if it were more conductive.

Ask yourself:

- What would be the key differences to the customer?
- What value and capabilities would the customer realize that they're not realizing now?
- What would the relationships at the customer interface look like?
- How would knowledge flow between our customers and us?

The primary purpose of the conductive organization is to create value for the customer, so it seems sensible to consider what becoming more conductive would mean to your customers. Once you've outlined your own assumptions, sit down with a number of your customers and ask the same questions.

Then ask yourself:

- What did we learn from our customers?
- How were their answers different from what we thought they would be?
- How good were we at looking through the lens of our customers?

4. How is customer capital being created within your organization?

We defined customer capital as: *the sum of all customer relationships.* These relationships are further described in terms of the depth (share of wallet), width (share of market), length (durability), and profitability of the organization's interactions with all its customers. We've argued that customer capital is the only means to increasing, on a sustainable basis, the organization's financial capital.

Consider the importance you believe your organization places on each element of the customer capital definition.

- What value on a scale of 0-10 would we give the four dimensions:
- Depth—share of wallet
- Width—share of market
- Length—durability
- Profitability—value created
- Do we place profitability above durability?
- Do we take a balanced approach to customer capital generation?

In considering customer capital, close attention should be paid to a clear understanding of the intangible elements of your relationships with your customers. Another useful exercise here is to map the tangibles and intangibles of your relationship with customers using a tool like ValueNet Works™. Understanding the intangible value in your relationships with customers can provide a clear sense of the value-adding, knowledge-based, and customer-facing capabilities that are strategically worth protecting and enhancing.

5. **How will your organization begin the process of transforming itself from a make-and-sell to a sense-and-respond organization?**

We've explained that we believe there is a compelling need for organizations to shift from a make-and-sell to a sense-and-respond perspective. It's not an easy task and requires that attention be paid to the entire customer, human, and structural capital approach to generating capabilities and creating relationships. An initial step may be to simply identify the major elements in the process by which your organization presently makes and sells products and/or services. Then describe what a sense-and-respond process might look like. By drawing these process maps, you can obtain an idea of where deeper relationships and new capabilities are required.

Understanding the differences between a sense-and-respond and a make-and-sell configuration is a starting point for your plan to become more conductive.

6. **For your organization, what will first-mover advantage look like in practice?**

The goal of a sense-and-respond organization is to place itself in line with or just ahead of market demands. Outpacing or lagging behind your customers is no recipe for success. With proper placement, organizations can secure the benefits of first-mover advantage.

Begin with an assessment:

- Does our organization have first-mover advantage?
- If so, where and why?
- If not, why not?
- Of our competitors, which would we consider to have first-mover advantage? What's their competitive edge over us?

Then ask yourself:

- What specific changes will we have to make to our organization to achieve first-mover advantage? What benefits will it provide?
- How will first-mover advantage improve our relationships with our customers? What will it mean in terms of customer capital generation?
- How important will first-mover advantage be to our employees? Will it be a badge of honor? How capable are our employees of delivering this advantage?
- What will our claim of first-mover advantage mean to our competitors? How capable are they of responding rapidly to displace us?

If you believe that claiming first-mover advantage is an absolute requirement (rather than being, for example, fast followers), then the next task is to determine how to use the first-mover goal as a standard around which to rally the organization. How will you build the capabilities to create this advantage?

7. How will you learn with your customers?

In the knowledge era, learning with the customer is crucial for understanding how the relationship required by the customer evolves and for building new capabilities for both the customer and the organization. We've explained that learning with the customer requires collaboration and listening skills within the organization. Nothing short of new forms of conversation are required.

Start by identifying examples of learning with your customers. What success stories can you tell? What horror stories can you learn from?

Then ask:

- How can we capture new knowledge from meetings with customers? Do employees have the required skills to learn with our customers? Do they have partnering mindsets and the capabilities to participate in active listening and analyze their findings?

- How are web-based processes being leveraged for the purpose of customer learning?
- How are customer surveys, focus groups, and values instruments being used to get to the kernel of customer concerns and aspirations?
- What do our customer service or call center representatives tell us? What does our analysis of customer interactions tell us?
- What processes are in place to ensure that the knowledge garnered from customers is stored, shared, and acted upon?

Being aware of how customer learning currently takes place can show you how much work has to be done to make learning with the customer a core capability in your organization.

8. How will you implement a branding strategy?

Shaping a corporate brand image that resonates with the values, aspirations, and desired experiences of customers and employees alike is key in a highly conductive organization. Internal and external branding is a powerful mechanism by which to cement relationships between employees and customers and to align the interests of both with those of the organization.

When we talk about branding, we don't differentiate between the customer and the employee. Both are equally important in creating a meaningful and durable branding strategy. Moreover, if the employees believe in and live the brand promise, they will be more inclined to deliver the brand promise to your customers.

Describe the brand promise your organization currently portrays to customers. Map employee experiences to all elements of that promise. This exercise will help you identify programs and initiatives needed to close any gaps between what the brand promises and what it actually delivers.

9. What would a conductive organization look like from the perspective of your employees?

It's important to see the conductive organization through the eyes of the customer. But it's equally vital to view it through the eyes of your employees. After all, conductivity relies on a high-quality connection between the customer and the employee.

Ask yourself:

- How many employees have direct contact with customers?
- How would employees characterize the nature of their relationships with customers?
- What capabilities do employees have to create and maintain high-quality relationships with customers?
- What's the quality of internal relationship? Do employees practice internally what they apply externally?
- Do employees have access to the information they need to do their work?
- Do employees participate in formal or informal knowledge exchange structures such as a community of practice?
- What do employees value about our organization?

Now, ask some employees these same questions and compare your perceptions with their reality. If there's a difference, what might you need to change in order to better align your two perceptions?

10. How do you develop strategy?

Strategy development is often considered a painful annual exercise that is quickly shelved once a high-gloss document is produced. In a highly conductive organization, the focus is on a comprehensive strategy-making cycle—on the act of creating strategy based on customer learning and collaboration, creating strategic symmetry, and aligning capabilities to realize the strategy's goals.

- To what extent is the leadership of our organization using strategy making as a tool to make meaning and develop coherence?
- What does strategy making look like in our organization? What is the level of commitment across the organization to our busi-

ness strategies? Who's involved in the strategy-making process? And, what happens once a strategy document is developed? Is there strong ownership throughout the organization for the objectives that are cascaded based on renewed business strategies? How can we find ways to include broader-based participation in strategy making?

- To what extent do our current strategies stem from an outside-in perspective?
- Are the current strategies fully utilizing the capabilities of the organization to create value for the customer or are they limited by the *bulkanization* imposed by the current structure?
- Do current business strategies and plans reflect existing patterns of performance as opposed to stretch goals that would bring to the fore new possibilities for the organization?
- How involved are our customers in our strategy-making process? What role do they play?
- Throughout the strategy-making process, how do we identify the capabilities that we'll require to realize our strategic goals? How do we know that we have the right mix for success?
- Have we identified our organization's strategic capabilities? What are they? What distinguishes us in our marketplace? Are we limiting what we have to offer our customers because we lack capability in given areas?
- Is the overall organization strategy conducive to successfully realizing our business strategies? What are the obstacles that might stem from our culture or our structure that stand in the way of having a more successful market presence?
- Do we have a knowledge strategy? How is it linked to other strategies? What capabilities should be targeted for development through the knowledge strategy? What do we have in place to increase the quality and speed of our knowledge flow?

11. **What is your culture today, and what do you want it to be in the future?**

Culture is a key organizational capability and an important component of an organization's structural capital. But it's also the one that is most often overlooked, misunderstood, and underutilized. Culture essentially dictates whether durable strategic relationships and capabilities can be created. Culture has deep roots. The first step is to define your organization's culture. It's a large-scale effort that requires a thorough analysis. If your organization hasn't completed a systematic review of its culture, you can begin by asking:

- How would we describe the collective mindsets that shape how the organization functions? How would we characterize how work is accomplished in our organization?
- Is there a climate of self-initiation? Will people take risks? If so, are they rewarded?
- What level of trust exists in our organization? At what level is it the strongest? At what level is it the weakest?
- How interdependently is our organization structured? Do cross-functional work teams exist? Are there formal or informal networks that run across departments?
- Do we have a partnership approach internally? Externally? Or both?

To obtain a 360-degree picture, ask your customers, employees, and partners to identify how they see your organization's culture. How would they describe the way things get done around your organization?

12. How does your organization foster a self-initiation culture?

In the knowledge era we need a new employment contract that is based on commitment, not on entitlement. The central agreement the individual makes in this contract of commitment is to create value in the organization in exchange for the ability to create capabilities for him- or herself. However, employees cannot fully make this commitment unless they are self-initiated.

There are a number of key tasks and/or mindset shifts that an organization can complete in order to create an environment conducive to self-initiation. For example, abandon any expectations of employee loyalty in return for a job-for-life and view the employee as a business of one. How pervasive is self-initiation in your organization?

Ask yourself:

- Do people have a sense of ownership for the value they create for the customer? In what key ways will a self-initiated culture deepen our customer relationships?
- How will self-initiated employees benefit our organization?
- What are the major structural barriers to self-initiation and how will we overcome them? What are the key management practices that reinforce dependency on the part of the employees?
- What are the major cultural barriers to self-initiation and how will we overcome them?
- In what key ways will a self-initiated culture deepen our relationship with customers?

Then ask your employees for their perception on this key culture component. Are your responses congruent?

13. How will you ensure that trust permeates all relationships?

Trust should permeate all relationships that the organization enters into—with customers, between partners, and among employees. Trust is essential to building the level of collaboration required for knowledge sharing. In short, trust is a necessary environmental condition for conductivity. The bandwidth of conductivity will be severely restricted where trust is diminished or absent.

Realistically consider the levels of trust the organization has with each of its stakeholder groups and how much trust they, in turn, have in the organization. Then, visualizing what high-trust relationships with and between groups would look like, outline how higher levels of trust might be achieved.

14. How will interdependence be achieved?

In a climate of high trust, all partners in a network relationship will be contributing capabilities and expect to generate new capabilities in a reciprocal way. What levels of interdependence exist in your organization? Profile several best practice situations. What are the common characteristics? What patterns can you identify?

15. How will you shape a culture based on partnerships?

Self-initiation, trust, and interdependence create a climate in which partnerships can flourish. Partnerships, whether short-term or long-term commitments and formally or informally structured, are the means by which value-added work gets done in the knowledge era. A key organizational capability is knowing how best to configure the organization so that partnerships can be assembled, disbanded, and reassembled with speed and focus. This process requires a deep understanding of how to identify complementarities between people, functions, or organizations.
Ask yourself:

- Does our organization use a team approach? If so, do the teams represent cross-functions?
- How do we build team capabilities?
- Do we participate in value-creation networks? If so, what do they look like? Can we identify common characteristics? If not, why not?
- Is our competition participating in value-creation networks? What's the effect on their ability to compete in our marketplace?
- Do we have a partnership relationship with our customers? If so, what does that relationship look like? If not, what would our

customers think if we approached them with the possibility of partnering?

16. By what process will you create the core values of the organization?

Effective partnerships require a base of shared values. Building a highly conductive organization requires the articulation of these core values that serve as a framework to guide all decision making and outline the expected behaviors within all of its relationships—internal and external.

Shaping core values must not simply be an exercise where the senior team gets together and decides what these values will be and then communicates them to employees and customers. Rather, core values should be created through the involvement of as many employees as possible.

By identifying employees' values, it becomes possible to see where major convergences are and create a culture to which most employees can relate and commit. The following questions may further define that process for your organization. Identifying values is a significant task that requires expertise and support tools. If your organization would undertake the necessary work, what do you think the core values might be? Gauge the readiness of your organization to undertake a values initiative.

- Do we have a champion of a values initiative? Do we have any internal expertise? What team would be responsible for managing the initiative?
- What would our executive team say are its core values?
- How would our organization's core values be viewed by our customers and partners? Would they share them?

17. What would a new leadership model look like in your organization?

There are significant differences between the leadership roles and behaviors required in the industrial era and those demanded in the knowledge era. You need to understand the leadership characteristics that can deliver the relationships you want with your customers, the brand you wish to create, and the culture and core values you wish to nurture in the organization. Consider how prevalent these leadership characteristics are within your organization and how you can close any gaps.

- How does our organization define leadership? Do we view leadership as a capability that should be developed and exercised in all employees?
- How would we rate the levels of capabilities for: detecting patterns, responding with speed, generating capabilities, creating partnerships, and infusing meaning?
- Is leadership devolved throughout our organization? Can we describe several best practice examples? What are their common characteristics?
- How will we ensure that leadership skills and responsibilities devolve deep within the organization?

18. What are the key ways that knowledge exchange will be facilitated within your organization?

Facilitating the free flow of tacit knowledge is critical in a highly conductive organization.

- What processes are in place to support knowledge flow in our organization?
- What approaches enable the delivery of high-quality knowledge?
- Do communities of practice exist in our organization? Are there strategic communities that we should develop?
- Is there a climate of trust in our organization that encourages knowledge exchange? Do we consider knowledge to be power?

- Do we have a technology infrastructure that could support knowledge access and exchange processes? If so, are these processes accessible by all employees? Do customers also have access?
- Have we mapped expertise networks? If so, what patterns have we noticed?
- How could expertise network maps drive improvements at the employee, organizational, and customer levels?

19. How will you leverage explicit knowledge within the organization?

Creating processes and leveraging technology to capture, codify, and store explicit knowledge and building systems that access, retrieve, and disseminate knowledge are critical to conductivity. Leveraging explicit knowledge as a strategic resource requires a comprehensive technology infrastructure to bring real-time learning to all employees' desktops.

- Does our organization view capturing explicit knowledge as a strategic imperative? If not, how will we create this urgency at the highest levels?
- What technology infrastructure can we leverage for accessing knowledge across the organization?

20. How will you reconfigure learning for the knowledge era?

Traditional approaches to training are no longer appropriate in the knowledge era. Industrial-era push-mode classroom-based models struggle to deliver the real-time, just-in-time, just-enough, and just-in-case learning requirements to the desktop. Learning needs to be delivered through pull-mode e-learning mechanisms. Think about how to create an environment in which e-learning is the organization's preferred approach to developing capabilities.

- What's the predominant approach to learning in our organization? Is it classroom based or available via a variety of channels? Is it an event or integrated into everyday work routines?
- Do employees know how to learn online? Has our organization built the generative capability to learn and collaborate at the employees' desktops?
- Does our organization provide a wide range of learning materials? Encourage mentoring and coaching? Have a variety of collaborative tools?
- Would employees accept the notion that work is learning? That the two go hand in hand?
- How will we shape a culture in which learning at the desktop is encouraged?
- Can customers access our learning resources?

21. Who will be the custodians of conductivity within your organization?

Industrial-era organizational structures are incompatible with requirements for rapid dissemination of knowledge and for team-based approaches. New configurations are needed to facilitate knowledge flow across the organization and between the customer and employees. Transformation to a highly conductive organization is everyone's responsibility, but it needs champions and stewards to ensure success. Who will be the custodians of conductivity in your organization?

- Does our present functional configuration limit our ability to become more conductive?
- How might we restructure our organization to enable conductivity?
- Who will be the champions of the transformation?
- Who will provide the vision?
- Who will implement the organizational capabilities required?

- How will we involve our customers in shaping the future organizational structure?

From Conductive to Highly Conductive

All organizations can be described as conductive to a certain extent. There's some level of information flow in every organization—that is, unless their organizational ECG registers a flatline! At the other end of the scale, the notion of *superconductivity* is equally unhealthy. It suggests a state of zero resistance, where knowledge would simply flow in one ear and out the other.

We've introduced a number of new ideas about how to achieve breakthrough performance in the knowledge era. We've suggested a new language for talking about new concepts. We've also proposed the Knowledge Capital Model as an overarching framework for visualizing how value is created today.

These ideas, language, models, and frameworks have evolved through our practical experience of leading corporations in today's evolving knowledge economy. The approaches we offer have worked for us, but we're certainly not presenting them as *the* final word on knowledge-era organizational configurations. This book is intended as a vehicle to share ideas for further experimentation, alongside other ideas that are emerging in the literature, at conferences, and in conversations between colleagues.

We expect that there'll be questions about the validity or robustness of what we propose. If we've initiated discussion about our work, then we'll have achieved what we originally set out to do—to begin a conversation about how the dynamics of successful 21st-century organizations can evolve.

Organizations that achieve breakthrough performance will be those that systematically work to expand their level of conductivity by generating new organizational capabilities. Conductivity itself functions through the quality and preparedness of the organization's generative capabilities, a term we use to describe an organization's ability to create new capabilities at the speed at which their customers require them. Generative capabilities are the outcome of a carefully orchestrated strategy to leverage the individual (attributes, competencies, mindset) and organizational (strategy, structure, systems, culture, leadership) capabilities of the organization.

A knowledgeable person recognizes that the more knowledge he or she amasses, the more there is to learn. The same is true of the conductive organization. We can see no limit to the value that being highly conductive brings to the customer, the employees, the organization, and its stakeholders. Breakthrough performance is within the reach of organizations that calibrate their strategy, culture, structures, and systems to the customer.

Working in full strength of its capabilities, striving for coherence, and calibrating to the customer, the highly conductive organization elevates the trajectory of its possibilities and narrows the variability of its financial performance. This organization surpasses itself. It's constantly stretching, relying on its strategy-making capabilities to break through current levels of performance, finding its aspirations achievable.

Glossary

Capabilities: *a collection of cross-functional elements that come together to create the potential for taking effective action.* These elements include: attributes, skills, knowledge, systems, and structures. Capabilities represent tangible and intangible components that are needed to enable performance. Capabilities are the link between strategy and performance.

Communities of practice: *groups of self-governing people whose practice is aligned with strategic imperatives and who are challenged to create shareholder value by generating knowledge and increasing capabilities.* We shaped this definition to illustrate self-initiation (self-governing) and clearly describe the strategic nature of such communities.

Conductive organization: *An organization that continuously generates and renews capabilities to achieve breakthrough performance by enhancing the quality and the flow of knowledge and by its strategy, culture, structure, and systems calibrating to the needs of its customers and the marketplace.*

Conductivity: *the capability to effectively transmit high-quality knowledge throughout the organization: from the customer interface across all functions, business groups, and project teams.*

Culture: *the sum of the individual opinions, shared mindsets, values, and norms within an organization.*

Customer capital: *the sum of all customer relationships,* defined as the depth (penetration or share of wallet), breadth (coverage or share of market), sustainability (durability), and profitability of the organization's relationships with all of its customers. While customer capital includes all external relationships, we focus on customers and suppliers—not all stakeholders. Our goal is to focus on people directly involved in value creation for the customer and the organization.

Customer facing: *people who or functions that interact directly with the customer through a variety of contact points or media.*

Customer interface: *the dynamics that take place between the customer and the organization—the touchpoints through which the organization and the customer interact.*

Explicit knowledge: *knowledge that has been articulated or codified in words or numbers, such as tools, procedures, and templates.*

Generalized reciprocity: *a state in which all parties (e.g., suppliers, customers, partners, employees) contribute something of value to the relationship and all parties also derive value from that relationship commensurate with their level of investment.* A mutual interest is identified, and a commitment to continue the relationship is made.

Generative capabilities: *capabilities that enable the continuous generation of other capabilities.*

Human capital: *the attributes, competencies, and mindsets of the individuals who make up an organization.* The individual capabilities of an organization serve to build organizational capabilities and create value for customers.

Individual capabilities: *the attributes, competencies, mindsets, and values of an individual within an organization.* A combination of the observable employee-applied knowledge, skills, and behavior in the workplace and the attitudes and values that guide that behavior.

Knowledge: *the capability to take effective action.*

Knowledge architecture: *the blueprint that outlines the approaches for placing the collective knowledge of the organization at the disposal of everyone.*

Knowledge strategy: *the strategy embedded in the organization, customer, and business strategies to build knowledge flow across the organization in a systematic way.* The knowledge strategy outlines how an organization will make knowledge accessible, provide channels of access and exchange across the organization, and increase its level of conductivity.

Leadership: *the manner in which individuals choose to exercise their responsibilities.* We purposely use individuals and not managers because we see leadership as a capability that must be encouraged and nurtured within all employees, not just the few who sit at the top of the organizational chart.

Learning: *the process of turning information into knowledge to take effective action.*

Organizational capabilities: *the strategies, systems, structures, culture, and leadership that make up an organization.* Organizational capabilities refer to the *know how* of the organization—the frameworks and platforms that support the ability of individuals to work effectively to make the organization a successful enterprise.

Strategic capabilities: *capabilities that are elevated to a strategic level because they are needed to meet objectives as outlined by the overarching business strategy.*

Strategy: *the amalgamation of an organization's objectives, including the broader goals and the actions necessary to accomplish them.*

Strategy making: *the constant renewal of strategy to align and keep pace with the evolution of customer and marketplace needs.* An organizational capacity to develop and implement strategies that expand the organization's strategic horizon—its opportunities to provide solutions that respond to customer needs.

Structural capital: *the strategies, structures, processes, culture, and leadership that translate into specific core competencies of the organization* (e.g., the ability to develop solutions, manage risk, engineer processes, understand markets). Organizational capabilities leverage individual capabilities in creating value for customers.

Tacit knowledge: *the intuitions, perspectives, beliefs, and values that result from the experience of individual employees and of the organization as a whole.*

Values: *the ideals that help individuals set priorities and guide behavior.* Values are held by individuals or organizations. When held in common, they're called core values.

About the Authors

HUBERT SAINT-ONGE

Hubert Saint-Onge is the Principal of SaintOnge/Alliance, a firm that works with organizations to increase their strategic capabilities. He is also Co-Chairman of Konverge Digital Solutions, a technology firm that specializes in providing solutions for knowledge work. For the past decade, Hubert has been refining the Knowledge Assets Framework – a model that integrates business plans with people management systems, using a technology architecture and organizational infrastructure. He is a respected advisor to Fortune 500 companies and a widely recognized leading practitioner in the field of knowledge management. Hubert is also the Executive in Residence in the Centre for Business, Entrepreneurship and Technology at the University of Waterloo in Ontario.

As the former Executive Vice President, Strategic Capabilities at Clarica Life Insurance Company, a key element of Hubert's mandate was to leverage the firm's business through the systematic application of knowledge management and learning organization principles. He was instrumental in developing the Clarica brand, which contributed directly to Clarica's three-fold market capitalization prior to its merger with Sun Life Financial.

A decade earlier, as Vice President, Learning Organization and Leadership Development for the Canadian Imperial Bank of Commerce (CIBC), Hubert's role was to support the accelerated development of capabilities required to achieve CIBC's business strategy. He developed the CIBC Leadership Centre from concept to reality, where with his team, integrated programs and tools aimed at changing organizational culture and building strategic focus were developed. This work was feature in a *Fortune* article as a prime example of how to accelerate organizational learning.

Hubert was identified as one of the five practitioners who have had the most impact on organizations in Davenport and Prusak's book, *What's the Big Idea? Creating and Capitalizing on the Best Management Thinking* (Harvard Business School Press, 2003) and interviewed in Chatzkel's book, *Knowledge Capital: How Knowledge-Based Enterprises Really Get Built* (Oxford University Press, 2003).

He is the co-author of *Leveraging Communities of Practice for Strategic Advantage* (Butterworth-Heinemann, 2003) as well as the author of numerous articles on generating capabilities, leadership development, knowledge value creation, and learning organizations.

Hubert holds an Honors BA in Political Science from York University (Toronto, Ontario) and an MA in Political Science Carleton University (Ottawa, Ontario) with specialization in international economic integration.

CHARLES ARMSTRONG

Charles Armstrong is the President of S.A. Armstrong Limited, a third generation family business that designs, manufactures, and distributes engineered fluid handling products such as pumps, valves, and heat transfer equipment. With plants in Canada, the United States and the United Kingdom, S.A. Armstrong Limited is known world wide for many pioneering products. Canary Wharf in London is one of the many prestigious buildings around the world that uses Armstrong capabilities and products.

Charles began his career in international banking with the Bank of Nova Scotia in their Western Hemisphere International Regional office. He later joined the World Corporation Group at Citibank where he was responsible for global matrix relations management for multinational customers.

In 1990, Charles became President in S.A. Armstrong Limited where he has spearheaded the transformation of the 60-year old company into a broad entrepreneurial organization committed to becoming a market leader though innovation and relationship building. To set the foundation for this vision, Charles began a series of initiatives designed to elevate the leadership qualities of all managers. He developed the Enterprise Capital Model to help facilitate a greater awareness of the importance of intangible assets. The model is used to illustrate how the interaction between assets (human, structural, and customer capital) is responsible for value creation. His understanding of knowledge management principles was integral to the company becoming an early adaptor of new technologies. As a result, the company has fully implemented BaaN ERP, i2 Supply/Order Fulfillment, Livelink collaboration and knowledge management software. The IT structure supports over 400 employees and thousands of customers fully engaged internationally over the Internet. The company's customers tie into its interactive knowledge base. Today, the Armstrong group of companies is one of the most culturally aligned in the global manufacturing sector.

Charles has been cited in numerous publications for his work in understanding and managing flows of intangibles in organizations. In 2003, Henley Management College in the UK profiled S.A. Armstrong Limited as part of its KM Best Practice Series for the construction industry. In 2002, and again in 2003, it was named one of the 50 Best Management Companies in Canada in a program sponsored by Deloitte&Touche, CIBC, Queen's School of Business and the National Post.

In 1997, Charles started Know Inc., a company engaged in distilling the learnings from the world's experts in knowledge management into toolkits that can be deployed in any organizational setting. The toolkits along with practitioner expertise help organizations develop conditions and programs to become more productive. Know Inc. has pioneered work in social network mapping and value network analysis in its organizational applications supported by software such as Knetmap™ and Value Networks™.

In 2000, Armstrong purchased and evolved Konverge Digital Solutions which, in combination with Know Inc., became ⟨KonvergeandKnow⟩. ⟨KonvergeandKnow⟩ is the first organization in the KM sphere to recognize the knowledge architecture, culture, and IT infrastructure integration as key to developing a conductive organization. It is a full service practitioner, providing support tools and software implementation primarily in the financial and highly complex and configured engineered products sectors. The company has specific expertise embodied in its Rapids™ technology for efficiently wrapping organizational capability around customers.

Charles received a B.Sc. (Engineering) from the University of Guelph (Ontario, Canada) and an M.B.A. in international business from the Ivey School of Business, University of Western Ontario (London, Ontario).

Index